Madagascar

Madagascar

BY Ettagale Blauer
AND Jason Lauré

Enchantment of the World
Second Series

Children's Press®

A Division of Grolier Publishing

NEW YORK LONDON HONG KONG SYDNEY
DANBURY, CONNECTICUT

Frontispiece: Relaxing on Nosy Be

Consultant: Zoe Crossland, M.A., University of Michigan

Please note: All statistics are as up-to-date as possible at the time of publication.

Visit Children's Press on the Internet: http://publishing.grolier.com

Book Production by Herman Adler Design Group

Library of Congress Cataloging-in-Publication Data

Blauer, Ettagale.
    Madagascar / by Ettagale Blauer and Jason Lauré.
      p. cm. — (Enchantment of the world. Second series)
    Includes bibliographical references and index.
    Summary: Describes the geography, plants and animals, history,
economy, language, religions, culture, sports and arts, and people
of the island nation of Madagascar.
    ISBN 0-516-21634-1
    1. Madagascar Juvenile literature [1. Madagascar.] I. Lauré, Jason.
II. Title. III. Series.
DT469.M26B53 1999
969.1—dc21   99-36878
                                                   CIP

GROLIER
PUBLISHING

Acknowledgments

Our sincere thanks go to our incredible driver and guide, Lala, who took us safely around the island and shared a lifetime of knowledge. Thanks also to Falisoa Ramasiarimanana, who brought her country's history to life for us at the King's Palace in Ambohimanga. We thank Hanitra for sharing not only her music but her culture; David Fox, the honorary consul of Madagascar in South Africa; and Monique Rodriguez at Cortez Travel. Thanks to Johannes van Kuijck, who permitted us to tour the Star Brewery and Bottling Company, and to all the many other Malagasy who treated us with tremendous courtesy and warmth.

Contents

Cover photo:
Avenue of
baobab trees

CHAPTER

Folk musicians

Back cover photo: Woman preparing fishnets

A World Apart

8

THE MAP OF THE WORLD IS LIKE A SUPER JIGSAW PUZZLE whose pieces have been tossed into the oceans. If you could pick out the pieces and push them together, you would see how nicely the east coast of Africa fits with the subcontinent of India. There's just enough room between them for the island nation of Madagascar.

Long ago, when these pieces were joined together, they formed part of a supercontinent known as Gondwanaland. Scientists estimate that this huge landmass broke up about 80 million to 120 million years ago, creating the continents of Africa, Asia, and South America. One small part broke away on its own—the island of Madagascar, the fourth-largest island in the world. Some people call it a "mini" continent. Madagascar's western coastline perfectly fits the eastern coastline of Africa where the nations of Mozambique and Tanzania are found.

The breakup of Gondwanaland started a process of evolution that resulted in Madagascar's unique plant and animal life. Species that came to

Opposite: **Researchers in Madagascar dig in a rock formation holding the fossilized remains of a large, extinct bird.**

Lemurs evolved in isolation on Madagascar.

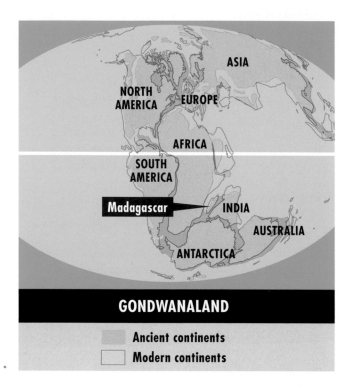

GONDWANALAND

Ancient continents
Modern continents

the island from Africa or Asia changed in different ways from their relatives that remained on those continents.

After the breakup, until human beings arrived there about 2,000 years ago, Madagascar developed in complete isolation. Its plants and animals evolved without outside influence. As a result, more than 90 percent of its natural environment is unique to Madagascar—it is found nowhere else on earth. Nearly all of the island's land mammals are found only on Madagascar. Its natural history has made Madagascar a kind of living laboratory, where evolution can be studied as a living science. On our visit to Madagascar, we'll meet these unique animals and see where and how they live. And we'll look at Madagascar's plant life, most of which is also unique—it is found nowhere else on earth.

Conservation

Some countries have conservation problems—but Madagascar *is* a conservation problem. The country's future is threatened by the same agricultural methods that feed its people.

When the first people came to Madagascar from Indonesia, they brought their basic food—rice—and their traditional method for growing rice—*tavy*. We call this

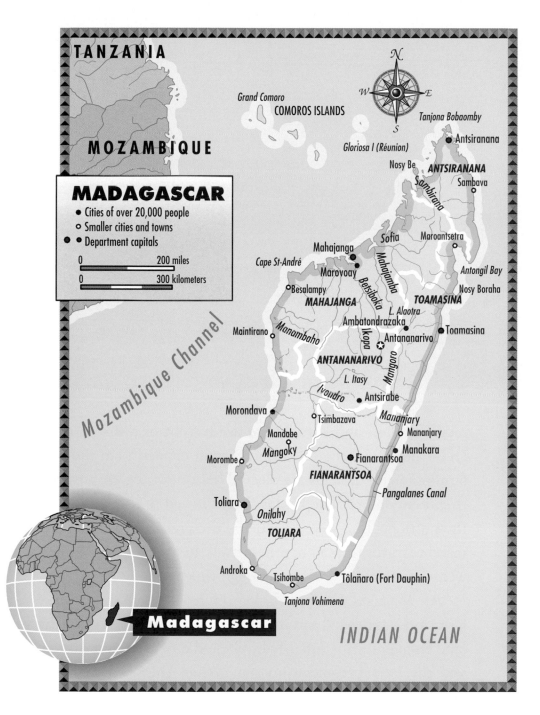

Geopolitical map of Madagascar

TANZANIA

MOZAMBIQUE

Grand Comoro

COMOROS ISLANDS

Gloriosa I (Réunion)

Tanjona Bobaomby

● Antsiranana

ANTSIRANANA

Nosy Be

● Sambava

MADAGASCAR
- ● Cities of over 20,000 people
- ○ Smaller cities and towns
- ● ● Department capitals

| 0 | 200 miles |
| 0 | 300 kilometers |

Mahajanga

Cape St-André

Marovoay

Besalampy

MAHAJANGA

Sofia

Maroantsetra

Antongil Bay

Nosy Boraha

TOAMASINA

L. Alaotra

Ambatondrazaka

Maintirano ○

Manambaho

Antananarivo

✪ Toamasina

ANTANANARIVO

L. Itasy

Ivondro

Antsirabe ●

Morondava ●

Tsimbazava ○

Mandabe

Mangoky

Morombe ○

Fianarantsoa ●

Mananjary ○

Manakara ●

FIANARANTSOA

Pangalanes Canal

Toliara ●

Onilahy

TOLIARA

Androka ○

Tsihombe ●

Tôlañaro (Fort Dauphin)

Tanjona Vohimena

Mozambique Channel

Mahajamba

Betsiboka

Ikopa

Mangoro

Sambirana

INDIAN OCEAN

Madagascar

Slash-and-burn farming has contributed to the destruction of Madagascar's rain forest.

method "slash and burn." Rice needs a lot of water to grow, and it needs soil that is rich in certain elements. In the tavy farming method, fields are cleared for a new rice crop by setting them on fire. The land is then allowed to rest and regain the nutrients that were used up by the previous crop. It takes many years for the soil to renew itself. In the past, the farmers were able to allow the land enough time.

As Madagascar's population increased, however, more farmland was needed and the farmers were not able to give the land enough resting time. They planted new crops more often, and the land became worn out. When they began to run out of flat land, which is the best land for growing rice, the farmers began to move into the forests. They used the same slash-and-burn method to clear the forests for planting.

Forests, especially rain forests, are rich in soils and nutrients, but they work best as forests. Every plant in a forest is there for

Southern Madagascar seen from the space shuttle *Endeavour*

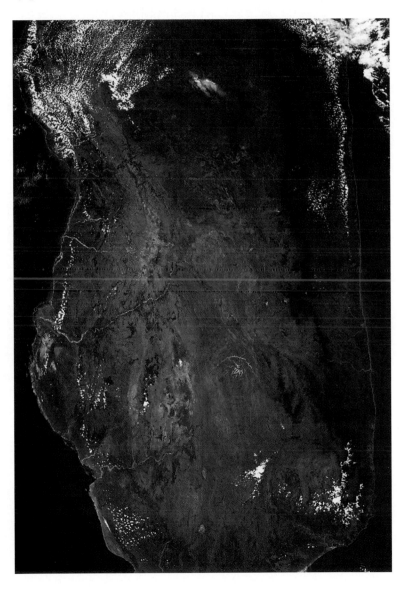

a reason, and each plant depends on the other plants around it. When the tall trees are cut down, sunlight pours in and burns the soil. Then, fires are set to clear the remaining growth. Once the land has been cleared in this way, there is nothing left to keep the soil in place.

Madagascar is often called the Great Red Island because of the deep red color of its soil. Each rainfall, however, washes the precious red top-soil down the hillsides. The mineral-rich soil eventually reaches the Indian Ocean and turns it red too. This phenomenon has been reported by astronauts, who say that, from space, the runoff of the red soil makes it look as if the island is bleeding to death.

Although the island is closest to Africa, it is believed that the first people of Madagascar came from Indonesia, more than 4,000 miles (6,437 kilometers) to the east. There are several theories about how and when people arrived on the island, but everyone agrees that the human population has dramatically changed Madagascar's animal and plant life. As a result, the island is losing animal and plant species at a rapid rate today. By one estimate, more than 85 percent of the original forest has been cut down for fuel, for sale, and for farming. Madagascar is now at the top of the World Wildlife Fund's list of endangered environments.

Logging is another contributor to the deforestation of the island.

The Malagasy, Madagascar's people, are mainly farmers. They know they are using up the only land they have, and this is a terrible dilemma for them. There is a Malagasy saying, *Tsy misy ala, tsy misy rano, tsy misy vary*, which means, "Without the forest, there will be no more water, without water, there will be no more rice." In spite of this understanding, the Malagasy don't know how to solve their problem. Tavy is the only way they know how to grow food. It is at the heart of their culture.

Rice fields cover every hillside in the central plateau.

Because Madagascar was a French colony at one time, many of its landmarks, cities, and other places are known by more than one name. When both Malagasy and French names are in use, this book will give both names, with the French name in parentheses.

Madagascar is a living textbook that its people are writing every day. Will they be able to save their island home before the land is used up? Will they learn what they need to know? What kind of farming methods do the Malagasy people use, and why are they so harmful to the environment? Can anyone from outside the country help the Malagasy save their land? Let's find out.

An Island of Contrasts

MADAGASCAR IS THE FOURTH-LARGEST ISLAND IN THE world, excluding the island-continent of Australia. It covers 226,660 square miles (587,004 square kilometers), which makes it slightly smaller than the state of Texas. Only the islands of Greenland, New Guinea, and Borneo are larger. Madagascar measures 976 miles (1,571 km) from Tanjona (Cape) Bobaomby in the north to Tanjona Vohimena in the south. It varies in width from east to west, but at its widest point—from near Lac Mandrozo on the west to Mahavelona in the east—it measures 360 miles (579 km).

Madagascar lies in the Indian Ocean about 250 miles (402 km) east of Africa. It is separated from the African continent by the Mozambique Channel. If you traveled all around Madagascar's coastline, you would cover about 2,600 miles (4,184 km). The eastern shore of the island is quite straight for most of its length and has harbors only in the northeastern part, while the western coast is irregular, marked by many inlets and bays.

Madagascar has a remarkably varied geography and climate. Each of its geographic regions is extremely different and because of this, each has its own plant and animal life. To picture Madagascar, think of a long mound of sand. Push the sand up from the right and left until it forms a high ridge in the center. This center spine is a chain of mountains that pushes up against a high plateau—a flat region. From this high

Opposite: **Small boats at harbor in the north**

plateau, the land slopes down into varied types of terrain. The mountain range also sets the stage for the different climates found on the island. Tropical forest is found in the east and

Farms blanket this part of Madagascar's high plateau.

north, for instance, while a forbidding desert lies in the south and southwest.

People disagree about how to divide Madagascar into geographical regions. Some say there are three regions, some say four, while still others divide the land into five regions. It may be easiest to think of the long island as three strips of land: the plateau in the center, the eastern coastal strip, and the western part with its plateaus and plains. A fourth region is the Tsaratanana Massif at the north end of the island. The highest point of the island, Maromokotro, which stands 9,436 feet (2,876 meters) high, is found here. The northern end has a natural harbor at Antsiranana (Diego Suarez). Nearby lies the island of Nosy Be (*nosy* means "island" in the Malagasy language).

The desert landscape of the south

Madagascar's Geographical Features

Area: World's fourth-largest island at 226,660 square miles (587,004 sq km)

Highest Elevation: Maromokotro Peak, 9,436 feet (2,876 m) above sea level

Lowest Elevation: Sea level along the Indian Ocean

Longest River: Mangoky, 350 miles (560 km)

Largest Lake: Alaotra, 70 square miles (181 sq km)

Greatest Annual Precipitation: 128 inches (325 centimeters) of rainfall, on the east coast

Lowest Annual Precipitation: 14 inches (36 cm) of rainfall, in the southwest

Highest Average Temperature: 84 degrees Fahrenheit (29 degrees Celsius), along the coast

Lowest Average Temperature: 5°F (-15°C) in the mountains

Greatest Distance North to South: 976 miles (1,571 km)

Greatest Distance East to West: 360 miles (579 km)

Coastline: 2,600 miles (4,184 km)

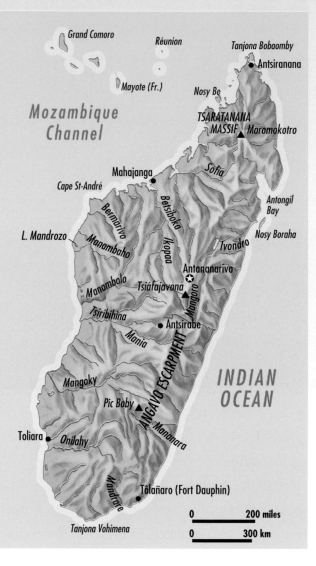

The eastern coastal strip is narrow, an average of 30 miles (48 km) in width. A remarkable waterway, the Pangalanes Canal (Lakandranon' Ampangalana), runs 400 miles (644 km) along the coast. The canal was formed naturally by a combination of ocean currents and sand washing up on the island until a lagoon was created. The land rises very sharply upward

The Pangalanes Canal

at a steep angle from the coast forming an escarpment—a flat-topped stretch of land. The escarpment continues for 800 miles (1,287 km) from north to south, almost the length of the island, forming a barricade between east and west. This barricade, called the Great Cliff, divides the island into two parts that are different in every way.

The trade winds that blow constantly from the east bring an almost steady spray of rain that sometimes comes down in sheets. This moist wind gives the region an enormous annual rainfall. The western zone is wider and drier, with coral reefs along the coastline. Tiny islands near the northwest end of the island are the tips of ancient volcanoes.

Madagascar's weather blows onto the island—from the east and from the west. The trade winds blow all year long but grow stronger from April to October. They are filled with moisture and bring the east coast of Madagascar up to 128 inches (325 centimeters) of rain each year—that's nearly a half-inch (1.3 cm) of rain every day! One of the areas that receives the most rain is Maroantsetra, on the Bay of Antongil. As the trade winds continue westward across the island, they lose their moisture.

The east coast receives heavy rainfall.

More rain comes from the monsoon winds that blow onto the northwest coast and the northern plateau. This hot, wet wind doesn't reach the southwestern part of the island, and neither do the trade winds. So, although there are two wet winds blowing onto Madagascar, both of them skip over the southern part of the island. As a result, the southwest has a climate almost like that of a desert. Rainfall varies all over the island. The northwest, around Nosy Be, receives 83 inches (211 cm) a year. Farther down the west coast, Maintirano receives 37 inches (94 cm) while Toliara (Tuléar), in the southwest, gets only 14 inches (36 cm) a year.

Madagascar has two seasons—a hot, wet season that usually begins in November and runs through March, and a cooler, drier season that runs from April through October. This varies by region. In the rainiest areas, the dry season lasts just a few weeks. Madagascar's climate is changing, however, like weather in other parts of the world. The wet season is starting later in the year.

July is the coolest month of the year, when temperatures range from 50°F (10°C) to about 78°F (26°C). December is the hottest month, with temperatures between 61°F (16°C) and 84°F (29°C). In both seasons, the warmest areas are at the coastline. As you go up into the hills, the temperature gets cooler. At night, it can be quite chilly in the mountains and in the capital city, Antananarivo, which is on the central plateau. At higher elevations, the temperature sometimes drops below freezing at night.

Cyclones

At the beginning of every year, tropical cyclones form far out over the Indian Ocean, usually starting in December or January and lasting until March. If they reach the east coast of Madagascar, they can bring sheets of rain so heavy that they blot out the view. The high rainfall also creates flooding in low-lying areas. Every few years, an especially severe cyclone hits the island, causing tremendous destruction and loss of life.

In February 1994, Geralda killed several hundred people on the east coast around Toamasina. It also destroyed the homes of a half-million people and severely damaged the railroad and roads along the coast. The financial cost of the damage was estimated at U.S.$45 million. In February 2000, Eline killed about 150 people, and the land suffered enormous damage. Rice fields and portions of the island's remaining forests were devastated. Flooding added to the threat of cholera. Because people who die of cholera must be buried quickly to prevent the spread of the disease, the cyclone may disrupt the traditional Malagasy burial rituals and weaken the people's close ties to their ancestors.

Raging Rivers

Madagascar has many rivers, most of them flowing down from the central highlands. The Mananara and the Mangoro flow to the east. The Maningory also flows to the east,

Washing clothes in the Ikopa River

Some rivers have
spectacular waterfalls.

beginning its journey in Lake Alaotra. Shorter rivers flowing
eastward include the Bemarivo, the Ivondro and the
Mananjary. They rush down the steep cliffs and often
form spectacular waterfalls. The Ikopa River flows past

Lake Andraikiba

Antananarivo and then joins the Betsiboka, which makes its way to Mahajanga on the west coast. Other west coast rivers are the Sambirano, the Mahajamba, the Mania, the Mangoky, and the Onilahy.

The Mandrare is the main river in the south. It is a seasonal river and is dry for months between the annual rainfalls. Several large lakes are found on the island, including Kinkony on the northwest and Lake Ihotry in the southwest. Lake Andraikiba, in Antsirabe, is known for its brilliant, clear blue water.

Coral Reef

Much of Madagascar's coast is rimmed with a coral reef. Coral is created by deposits from tiny sea creatures called polyps. The coral reef protects the beach from the ocean waves. If the reef is destroyed, the beach would be washed away. This is happening in several places around Madagascar. The reef also provides a safe harbor for fish that feed within the coral itself.

To protect the island, it is important to protect the coral reef. Many reefs near Malagasy villages are now damaged and dying. People in some villages use the beach as a toilet because they have no sanitation system. Human waste smothers the coral reef nearest to the village and creates a break in the reef, allowing the tide to wash over the beach. This destructive cycle leads to loss of the beach itself.

Looking at Madagascar's Cities

Toamasina, on Madagascar's east coast, is the country's second-largest city and its main seaport. Coffee, cloves, pepper, sugar, vanilla, and graphite are the chief products shipped from Toamasina. The city's main imports are machinery, textiles, and food. Industries in Toamasina include food processing and metalworking. The Betsimisaraka are the city's major ethnic group. They enjoy warm weather year-round. Toamasina's 128-inch (325-cm) annual rainfall is among the country's highest.

Antsirabe, Madagascar's third-largest city, is located in the Ankaratra Mountains in central Madagascar. Antsirabe has been known for its mineral springs since its founding in 1872 by missionaries from Norway. The name Antsirabe meaning "the place of much salt," refers to the salt left on the ground when water from the mineral springs evaporates. Because many people from the Merina ethnic group practice their skills as jewelers in Antsirabe, the city is also known as the Gem Capital of Madagascar.

Trade, shipping, and industry have helped Mahajanga become Madagascar's fourth-largest city. Mahajanga is located on Bombetoka Bay on Madagascar's northwest coast. The bay provides protection from cyclones and provides a deep, natural harbor. This harbor makes Mahajanga the nation's main seaport on the west coast. The city's chief industries are meat-canning and the manufacturing of sugar, soap, and cement.

Fianarantsoa, Madagascar's fifth-largest city, was founded in 1830. It is located in the southeastern highlands at about 4,000 feet (1,200 m) above sea level. Forests surround Fianarantsoa's upper and lower sections. This city is in the center of Madagascar's wine- and tea-producing area, and the Betsileo people also farm rice nearby.

A Place Like No Other

THE PLANTS AND ANIMALS OF MADAGASCAR LOOK AS IF they were drawn and colored by a very imaginative artist. Because they are almost all unique to the island, we are much less familiar with them than we are with the plants and animals of the African mainland, just a few hundred miles away.

Madagascar's plants and animals developed in isolation, so certain species of animals survived that would have not made it elsewhere. The animal that symbolizes Madagascar is the lemur. Ninety percent of all the lemurs in the world are found

Opposite: **A ring-tailed lemur carrying her baby**

Below left: **Thirty species of lemurs live in Madagascar.**

Below right: **A blue heron in Périnet Special Reserve**

only on Madagascar, and the rest live on the nearby Comoro Islands. Lemurs are related to the primate family of apes, monkeys, and human beings. They look a bit like monkeys, though they are only very distant cousins. Lemurs survived on Madagascar because they had little competition among primates and few other natural enemies.

Each of the thirty species of lemurs found on Madagascar lives in a particular area of the island. Most lemurs spend their time in the treetops, leaping from tree to tree, but some live mainly on the ground. Like people, lemurs have the all-important opposable thumb, but they have thumbs on their feet as well as on their hands. This gives them four ways to grip branches and food. Each species of lemur enjoys a different diet, which makes the loss of a habitat even more threatening. A lemur transplanted from one part of the island to another would be unable to find any familiar foods to eat.

The mouse lemur, as its name suggests, is the smallest lemur. Not only is it the smallest lemur, it is also the smallest primate on earth. It looks a lot like a mouse but is much smaller, sometimes weighing as little as 1 to 2 ounces (28 to 56 grams). It could easily fit into your hand. There are more mouse lemurs than any other species of lemur. Some naturalists believe there are more mouse lemurs than people on Madagascar.

The largest lemur on Madagascar is the indri, a handsome animal with a furry black-and-white coat. Indris weigh about 15 pounds (7 kilograms). They leap gracefully from tree to tree, using their long, powerful lower legs as springboards. When they land, they catch a branch with their feet, which

Lemur Lore

The ring-tailed lemur is the best known of the lemurs. It gets its name from the rings on its long furry tail. It is monkeylike in appearance, with long arms and legs. Because the ring-tail lives mainly on the ground, it is the most familiar of the lemurs. Visitors to Berenty Reserve often find themselves surrounded by ring-tails that climb over their vehicles and race across the sandy ground around visitors' feet. Ring-tails live in troops of about twenty animals. The ring-tailed lemur is also found in many zoos around the world and has become the symbol of Madagascar. Like the other lemurs, the ring-tail has very bright eyes that make it look as if it is staring at you.

Perhaps the strangest-looking lemur is the rare and shy aye-aye (above). Nature writer Hilary Bradt says, "The aye-aye seems to have been assembled from the leftover parts of a variety of animals." It has teeth like a rodent's, eyes like an owl's, a bushy tail like a fox's, and ears like a bat's. The aye-aye uses its big ears like radar, listening for tiny insects and worms moving inside a tree. It is such an odd-looking animal that Malagasy people in rural areas are afraid of it. The aye-aye is nocturnal, which means that it moves around only at night. Because it is so hard to find, for some years it was thought to be extinct.

are shaped just like human hands. The local people know the indri as *babakoto*, which means "cousin to man" in Malagasy. Because of their belief in this close relationship, it is forbidden to kill indris.

Although Madagascar is known today for its many unique species of animals, some have become extinct. What does it mean when we say that an animal is extinct? It means that we will never see that animal alive again—the species has died out. Some animals that are extinct in their natural habitat still survive in zoos, but others became extinct before people began saving them in zoos. Animals may become extinct because they cannot survive changing conditions. Many animals in Madagascar eat only certain plants that grow in small areas of the island. These are called "specialized" animals because they depend on special kinds of food.

Eggs of the extinct elephant bird are still found in southern Madagascar.

Before people came to Madagascar, there were much larger lemurs, including one as big as a gorilla. As many as fifteen lemur species are known to have become extinct since people first arrived on the island about 2,000 years ago. An amazing bird species—the elephant bird—became extinct only about 500 years ago. This bird, the largest that ever lived, had the shape of an ostrich but was much bigger and much heavier. It stood 10 feet (3 m) tall. Like the ostrich, it did not fly—its body size and shape were simply too big for its wings to lift it off the ground. We know the elephant bird existed because its enormous eggs are still sometimes found in southern Madagascar.

Changing Color

Half of all the chameleon species in the world are found only on Madagascar. Chameleons are small members of the reptile family. They are known for their ability to change color to blend in with the environment. They can turn green when standing on a leaf, or brown on a tree trunk. But chameleons actually change color to look more threatening when they feel they are in danger or when they want to impress a potential mate. They express their feelings by making their body color very bright and intense.

Chameleons have the scaly skin common to reptiles, but they're usually much more colorful than other reptiles. The panther chameleon has eyes outlined in orange and turquoise, which confuses predators. Those eyes can swivel 180 degrees, so that a chameleon can see everything without having to move its head and give away its position. Many chameleons,

A Parson's chameleon

such as the Parson's chameleon, have a long tail that curls round and round into a tight coil like the tail of a seahorse. This tail is very useful for holding onto a branch. It also helps with balance.

Chameleons may stay motionless on a tree branch, waiting for some unsuspecting insect to come along. Then, with the flick of a tongue, the insect is captured. This movement is so fast that you can't even see the insect disappearing. The tongue of a Parson's chameleon is as long as its entire body. This gives it a tremendous advantage in picking insects off a branch. The chameleon can be so far away that an insect doesn't even realize it's in danger until it's too late.

Arrival of the Animals

When large animals, including elephants, lions, and rhinos, were developing on the African continent, Madagascar had already broken away from the mainland. How did Madagascar's small animals arrive on this uninhabited bit of land? It is believed that they migrated from East Africa, floating across the Mozambique Channel on rafts of foliage. This means of travel ruled out large animals.

The mammals that made it to Madagascar and then evolved into their unique, present-day forms are much smaller than mammals on the African mainland. Madagascar's largest predator is the fossa. It is related to the mongoose, but it lives a life much like that of a small panther. It has the tawny coloring of a puma, and it hunts birds and small mammals. The fossa lives in a wide variety of Madagascar's climates including the rain forest, the dry forest, and the desert.

A male fossa in Kirindy Forest

Humpback Whales

Each year, humpback whales take an enormous detour in the Indian Ocean to reach the waters off Madagascar's northeast coast. Here, usually in August, the whales congregate in a great mating ritual. The area around Antongil Bay has become known as their hunting grounds.

Howard Rosenbaum, a researcher with the American Museum of Natural History, identified 250 individual whales in just two seasons. These huge creatures sometimes propel their entire enormous bodies out of the water—and no one knows why. Humpbacks travel 4,000 miles (6,437 km) each way on their annual migration.

Island Greenhouse

The unique animals of Madagascar look and act the way they do because of their natural environment, and the island's plant life is as unique as its animals. Most of it does not exist anywhere else in the world. There are so many species of plants that some are disappearing before they can even be named or recorded by scientists. More than 8,000 kinds of plants are found on Madagascar.

Rain Forest

Of all the regions in Madagascar, the eastern rain forest is home to the greatest number of animal and plant species. The plentiful rainfall encourages the growth of plants that cling to one another, curling and wrapping themselves together until it's difficult to see where one plant ends and another begins.

The tropical rain forest in Madagascar was once an unbroken band of greenery that stretched from Iharana (Vohémar) in the north to the very southern end at Tôlañaro (Fort Dauphin). Three human activities have broken up this band of greenery, leaving the remaining rain forest standing like green islands in the midst of barren land. First, some rich forestland was destroyed when it was cleared for farming by the tavy, or slash-and-burn, method.

Second, the timber industry, which cuts down trees for export, wiped out large areas of forest. Madagascar was known for its beautiful ebony, rosewood, and sandalwood trees. These woods are highly valued for furniture and sculpture, especially in Europe and the United States.

The rain forest is home to most of Madagascar's wildlife.

Finally, trees were cut down to be turned into charcoal, which is used locally for cooking. Eighty percent of the country's fuel for cooking and other domestic needs comes from wood and charcoal.

Small areas of rain forest remain in the north and the northwest. Some of it has been set aside as reserves or national parks in an effort to protect the remaining forest and its wildlife. The rain forest is divided into lowland and montane forests. The lowland rain forest is found at altitudes below 2,625 feet (800 m), while the montane forest is higher up, at altitudes between 2,625 feet (800 m) and 4,265 feet (1,300 m).

It's hard to say just how many kinds of orchids there are in Madagascar—more are being discovered all the time. They grow in very remote areas, often deep inside the remaining forests. The orchids that grow along the east coast live on tree branches—they don't even need soil. They are hidden from view, clinging to trees high off the ground. Even so, at least 1,000 species of orchids have been discovered. Others may become extinct even before they are found.

Orchids grow all over the island. To get an idea of the variety, a visitor would have to travel to many distant points. In the highlands, orchids tend to grow along the ground, in soil or in leaves at the base of trees. Some are quite small, but a few are large and showy like the orchids we see in corsages. Entire books have been written about Madagascar's orchids.

An orchid growing on a tree trunk in the rain forest

Baobab trees near Toliara

Baobab Trees

There is a strange type of tree in Madagascar that seems to have been put into the ground upside down. It is the baobab, which the Malagasy call *Reniala* or "Mother of the Forest." Although one species of baobab tree is well known in East Africa, there are seven species of baobab trees on Madagascar.

Baobabs are believed to live for thousands of years. They have huge trunks, without any branches except at the very top. These huge trunks are used to store water, which keeps the trees alive during dry periods. For this reason, some baobabs are known as "bottle trees." The branches grow up from the top of the tree and are very spidery looking, like roots.

A National Symbol

Madagascar has many unique plants, but one stands out because the Malagasy consider it the most important. It is a palm tree called *ravinala*, which means "forest leaves" in Malagasy. In English it is called the traveler's palm. Its long, feathery leaves spread out like a fan, and the base of its leaf stalk holds a supply of water. It is called the traveler's palm because it is always supposed to grow along an east–west direction. However, the trees don't seem to know about this, and they actually grow in all sorts of directions. The traveler's palm is well known around the world and can be seen in many botanical gardens. It is related to the banana tree. The tree is part of the national seal of Madagascar.

This is what makes the trees look as if they are growing upside down. Some baobabs grow up to 128 feet (39 m) tall. The Bontona, or Ringy baobab, has a trunk that can reach 49 feet (15 m) in diameter and store up to 30,000 gallons (113,562 liters) of water.

Baobabs are found in western Madagascar, where patches of forest remain. The giant baobabs at Morondava, on the west coast, are found in the dry forests. A road, "The Avenue of the Baobabs," is named for them. Some baobab trees produce fruits that the local people like to eat. To get to the fruit, they drive wooden spikes into the smooth tree trunks and then climb up. The bark of the baobab tree can be stripped off and used to make thatch for roofs. Parts of the tree are also used to make medicines and rope.

Nature Reserves

Madagascar is trying to preserve the natural environment that remains on this island-nation where every inch of land is precious. At the same time, officials are trying to revive some areas that have been overused. One result of this effort is a complicated system of parks and reserves. Areas under protection fall into six categories. The first category is "strict nature reserves." This includes four areas that have been set aside to be used for scientific research. A second group is made up of the six national parks: Ranomafana, Amber Mountain (Montagne d'Ambre), and Isalo, as well as Périnet-Analamazaotra and Mantadia, which together form Andasibe National Park. These parks are open to the public, although visitors must apply for permits. About twenty special reserves have been created around the country for the protection of threatened species or ecosystems.

Malagasy college students are now studying the environment of their own country, a very important step in

Isalo National Park

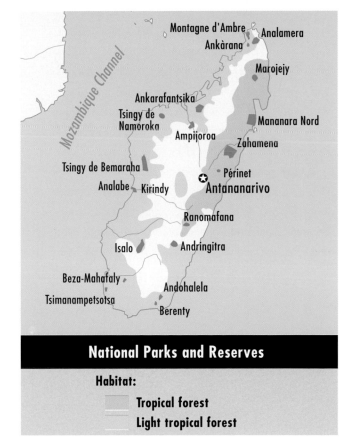

National Parks and Reserves

Habitat:

Tropical forest

Light tropical forest

Périnet Special Reserve

Périnet is a small reserve, but it is important because it is a refuge for the indri (right), the largest lemur. Périnet is within a three-hour drive from Antananarivo, Madagascar's capital city, on a winding mountain road that climbs through a rain forest. The reserve itself is very wet, and the trail through it is always wet. Visitors are led by a guide (above) who keeps track of the indris and knows where to find them. The animals also give a very good clue to their whereabouts—they make a shrill cry, almost a wail, which is a signal to other troops of lemurs. The cry can be heard for up to 2 miles (3.2 km).

It takes some skillful tracking to find the indris. But then it's just a matter of standing very still in the thick forest, looking up to the treetops, and there they are—beautiful black-and-white creatures with bright eyes and faces like teddy bears. The lemurs leap easily from

branch to branch and disappear from sight all too soon. But looking at the indris for those few minutes is worth the hike into the forest.

conservation. When local people become involved, it is easier to find solutions and to convince them to change some of their practices. In Périnet Special Reserve, college students walk with their teacher to study the role of the rain forest, the way it supports the lemur population, and to consider the impact of the loss of rain forest on their future.

Setting aside land for a reserve, no matter which category it falls under, is just the beginning. Each reserve needs special attention that suits its environment. It needs access roads and trained guides, which take time and money to create. Fees paid by visitors help with the funding, but the number of visitors to Madagascar is quite small. Also, the needs of the local people must always be considered. Parks take years to develop, and people must continue with their farming.

World Heritage Site

In a country where so many sites need protection, the United Nations agency UNESCO has chosen one for special attention. In 1990 it made Tsingy de Bemaraha Strict Nature Reserve a World Heritage Site—a place that both needs and deserves protection. Tsingy de Bemaraha is a strange kind of nature reserve because it is almost impossible for people to visit it. Over thousands of years, wind and water have eroded the landscape into a frightening "forest" of limestone spires as high as 66 feet (20 m). Each has been carved to a sharp point, and together they form an impenetrable maze. These spires are called *tsingy* in Malagasy. Some people believe *tsingy* means "to tiptoe," or "they hum." Both meanings describe the unique qualities of the tsingy.

Tsingy de Bemaraha is the largest protected area in all of Madagascar. It covers 375,871 acres (152,115 hectares). Because the area is so difficult to explore, it has not been widely studied. The list of its wildlife is constantly increasing. Fifty-three species of birds and six species of lemurs have been recorded so far. It is possible to see some of the landscape on a canoe trip on the Manambolo River, which runs through the reserve. Trips to the reserve are limited to the dry season—from April to November—and visitors must be accompanied by a guide. Tsingy are found in other parts of the western plateau, including Ankarana Special Reserve on the extreme northwest part of the island.

Euphorbia and didieracea bushes in Berenty Reserve

Berenty Reserve

The most successful park and the oldest nature reserve on Madagascar is Berenty, near the southern tip of the island. The land was set aside by Henri de Heaulme and his brother Alain, who were sisal planters during the French colonial period. Henri's son Jean has joined the family in looking after Berenty. As you approach the park, traveler's palms and baobabs are seen here and there. Close to Berenty, the landscape changes. Spiky euphorbia and didieracea bushes stand up all over, giving the nickname "spiny desert" to the region along the southern coast from Morombe to Fort Dauphin.

Several species of lemur live in Berenty, including brown, ring-tailed, and sifaka lemurs. The ring-tails spend a lot of time on the ground and have become used to people. The sifaka is a tall white lemur that seems to dance across the ground on its hind legs. The River Mandrare runs through the reserve, creating an oasis within this very dry region. Berenty is also home to about 100 species of birds.

Tsimbazaza

Tsimbazaza is a cultural center in Antananarivo that includes the country's only zoo, a museum, and a botanical garden. Since the center was founded it has struggled to find enough money to support its projects. You might wonder why Madagascar needs a zoo when the entire country has such incredible wildlife and plant life. But most Malagasy do not have the chance to travel around their own country. For them, the zoo is the best place to see it.

One of the main goals of the center is to conserve Madagascar's wildlife. Many species of lemurs live at the zoo, but they are kept in small cages and have devel-oped some very nasty habits. Lemurs in the wild are quite gentle and friendly toward people. The museum also has the skeletons of several animals that are now extinct, including the giant lemur and the elephant bird.

The botanical garden (above) is a beautiful part of Tsimbazaza. Because it is located in the heart of the city, it is quite easy for Malagasy to visit. Entrance fees for local people are very inexpensive, while foreigners are charged more. Two groups of lemurs live in the garden, each on its own small island full of trees, perches from which they can swing, and a place where visitors can see them without disturbing their lives.

A New Land

THE HISTORY OF HUMAN LIFE ON MADAGASCAR IS AMONG the shortest history of any people on earth. Madagascar was among the last places on the planet with a pleasant, fertile environment to be settled. After the island broke away from Gondwanaland, its plant and animal life developed without any human influence. No traces have been found of ancient people—no ancient bones, no fossil remains. Since the island is so close to East Africa, where bones of some of the earliest human beings have been found in several locations, we know that Madagascar broke away very early in the development of the world.

Left alone, the amazing plant and animal forms continued to evolve and to flourish. It is believed that people from Indonesia and Malaya began to arrive on the island about 2,000 years ago. The distances were vast, and the people probably did not travel directly across the open ocean. They most likely came in outrigger canoes, hugging the coastlines of the land areas they passed, traveling first along the coast of southern Asia and then the Arabian Peninsula until they reached the coast of East Africa. Eventually, a small group arrived on Madagascar. These early travelers took advantage of the winds and currents of the Indian Ocean, which flow eastward in one season and westward in the other season, allowing for round-trip travel.

Opposite: **The original inhabitants of Madagascar may have traveled there in outrigger canoes similar to this one.**

The slave market in Zanzibar, on Africa's east coast

The ancestors of this Merina woman may have come from Indonesia.

Later, Africans were probably brought to the island as part of the slave trade that was developing before the seventeenth century. Eventually, some Africans married into the Indonesian population. The final wave of settlers, today's Merina people, probably came from Indonesia as recently as 700 to 800 years ago. Over the centuries, all of these people came together as the Malagasy. Two proofs of the Indonesian origins of the Malagasy people are their musical instruments and their custom of building terraced rice paddies.

Each group brought its own customs and beliefs to the new land. Although they came from such different regions, they have two things in common today.

They all speak the same language—Malagasy—and they all believe in the power of their ancestors.

Early Visitors

Although Madagascar was settled late in human history, we know very little about when each group arrived or how many people came during the early waves of immigration. Early travelers made the island an important stop on their journeys. Traders from the Middle East, Asia, and Africa made regular stops there. The remains of forts built by Arab traders dating back to the ninth century show that the island was known to these skillful sailors more than 1,000 years ago. The forts are not the only reminders of these early visitors. Traces of the Arabic language can be found in Malagasy words relating to the cycle of the months and the days of the week.

European exploration of Madagascar's coast began about 1500 with the Portuguese, perhaps the best navigators of that time. Their advanced skills allowed them to sail the world's oceans and return safely home. Although the Portuguese were excellent sailors, historians believe that they first found Madagascar when a storm blew them off course. A Portuguese map drawn in 1502 places the island correctly in the Indian Ocean and labels it Madagascar, but we don't know where the name came from.

The Malagasy did not use that name. They called the island *izao tontolo izao*, which means "the whole world." They also called it *ny anivon 'ny riaka*, which means "in the midst of the waters." These two names help us understand how the Malagasy see themselves.

Harvesting Peppers in Madagascar, an illustration to Marco Polo's Book of Wonders

First Contact

The famous explorer Marco Polo, who made his great travels in the thirteenth century, wrote about Madagascar centuries before any European actually set foot there. The first European to touch the Madagascar shore was Diego Dias, a Portuguese explorer who arrived with a fleet in 1500. Other early European travelers to Madagascar met with a rough reception—from either the ocean or the people. The rough waters around Madagascar sank many ships and washed some sailors ashore. No one knows if they were killed by the local people, or if some of them remained on the island and lived out their lives as part of Malagasy families. Nearly a century later, when other Portuguese arrived and tried to convert the people to Catholicism, they were angrily rejected. The Portuguese gave up the idea of settling on the island in order to spread their religion. Instead, they continued to use it as a trading post and as a place to get fresh food and water on their journeys to the Far East.

The British Arrive

Ships of the British East India Company, one of the most aggressive trading companies of that time, also made their way

A ship of the British East India Company

to Madagascar during the seventeenth century, picking up supplies during their long journeys to the East. The British had another reason for coming to Madagascar, though. They had been told that this distant and isolated island was a treasure chest of riches just waiting to be claimed—that it had all kinds of metals the British wanted. This exciting idea, which had no truth in it at all, came from the imagination of a poet named George Herbert, who had never been there. Another book, published in 1640, claimed that the island was full of gold, silver, pearls, and precious stones. Its author had never been there either.

Although these dramatic descriptions had no basis in fact, they inspired a shipload of English people to establish a colony on the island. They were long on navigation skills and short on common sense. After arriving in Madagascar and building a fort, they were asked by a group of local people for their help in a battle. When the English refused to help, most of them were killed. They left behind the fort, now in ruins, and a large cemetery. For the moment, English dreams and schemes for Madagascar were at an end.

The French Arrive

The first French efforts to settle the island and convert the people were not much more successful than the British. Then, in 1648, the French East India Company sent Étienne de Flacourt to Madagascar. Although his tiny settlement at Fort Dauphin was in a state of constant war with the Antanosy people, Flacourt observed and recorded the people and their

Pirate Haven

Although the Europeans who wanted to establish settlements were not having much luck on Madagascar, another group of visitors was doing much better—the pirates who roamed the waters along the coast. The two major local groups on the island, the Merina and the Sakalava, were friendly to the pirates. The pirates didn't want to settle on Madagascar, they just wanted to use it as a base to attack and rob passing ships, so the local people allowed them to live there. The pirates came from England, France, and the Americas. Some of the world's most notorious pirates, including Captain Kidd, made their way to Madagascar.

way of life. He wrote the first important descriptions of the island and made a written record of the Malagasy language. He was under no illusions, though. When he left the island, he left a message for anyone who might follow: "O new arrival, read our warning, and it will save your life. Beware of the inhabitants. Farewell."

Warfare was a way of life for the French who arrived throughout the seventeenth century. Although some explorers and hopeful settlers made their way into the interior, their aggressive behavior angered the Malagasy. The end of this round of settlement attempts came in 1669, when the last settlers fled to the neighboring island of Réunion (then known as Île Bourbon). From Réunion, the French claimed the right to rule Madagascar—a strange claim when they had been totally unable to establish any kind of settlement there. The claim instead was based on land grants that were "given" by the French king to the French East India Company. Thus began a legal argument that went on for 200 years, until the French made Madagascar a French colony in 1896.

At the time of the first European attempts to settle Madagascar, the local people had organized themselves into three main kingdoms, each occupying a separate part of the island. The geography of the island allowed each group to develop separately, influenced both by the local climate and growing conditions and by its own traditions. The Merina people occupied the highlands, the Menabe lived in the west, and the Betsimisaraka occupied the east.

The Betsimisaraka were the most racially mixed group. Living near the coast, they were in contact with Europeans, including the pirates who used the island as a base. Once the European and American pirates had been stopped by an English fleet, the Betsimisaraka took up this profitable trade. They were skilled sailors who could paddle quickly through the water in their dugout canoes, which held as many as fifty men.

The Merina developed very much on their own. They were not affected by the invasions taking place in the other kingdoms, especially along the coastlines. One of the most important elements in their political development was the *fokonolona* village council. The councils were run by the

Jean Laborde

In the 1800s, a Frenchman named Jean Laborde changed the very nature of Malagasy society. He set up a factory at Mantasoa to produce iron for guns. The factory employed 1,000 workers. Under his guidance, the town grew into an industrial center where all sorts of goods were produced, including glass, pottery, bricks, and tiles.

Laborde also built a wooden palace for the queen in 1830. This massive work was later covered with stone by James Cameron, one of his main helpers. Most remarkable, Laborde manufactured lightning conductors, which are vital during the first months of the year when tropical storms cause much damage in the region around Imerina.

village elders and those considered to be high-born. The Merina population had three levels. First came the nobles, or high-born class. Next came the commoners, and third were the slaves they kept for their own use.

Merina Take the Lead

The Merina people grew into a powerful kingdom under their ruler, Andrianampoinimerina. This forceful leader conquered other people living on the island and brought them together under his leadership. He ruled from 1787 to 1810. He had extraordinary power because the people believed he ruled by divine right—that his power came from god.

He distributed land for each family's rice fields and made sure they could grow enough rice to give some to the king. He also organized the people to build canals to irrigate the crops. He was far-sighted in his planning. He did not allow the people to burn the forests. His dream of expanding his kingdom continued under his son,

King Andrianampoinimerina

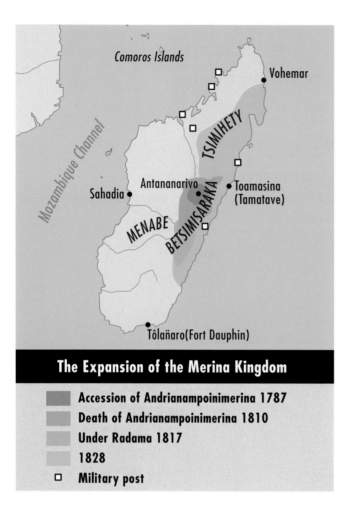

The Expansion of the Merina Kingdom

Accession of Andrianampoinimerina 1787
Death of Andrianampoinimerina 1810
Under Radama 1817
1828
□ Military post

King Radama I, who ruled from 1810 to 1828. Andrianampoinimerina would often say, "*Ny riaka no valamparihiko*," meaning "The sea is the limit of my rice field." To expand his kingdom, he conquered peoples from the highlands to the coast and gained control over the Betsileo and the Sakalava.

By the time King Radama I took power, Britain had recognized Madagascar as an independent country. The two had good relations, and Britain supplied weapons to Radama I. The king used these weapons to conquer most of the island and amassed an army of 35,000 soldiers. The people of the east coast were powerless to resist such a huge, well-armed force.

Radama I brought more than warfare to the Malagasy people though. Under his leadership, the British brought teachers to the island as well as a written language that used the Roman alphabet. The Protestant London Missionary Society established schools and churches. During its stay, the society converted nearly a half-million people to Protestantism. It also wrote down the Malagasy language using the Roman alphabet and brought literacy to the local people. Some students were sent to Britain for further education. A remarkable number of children, 164,000 of them, attended the mission's primary schools.

British Influence Ends

These productive years for the Merina were followed by a series of ups and downs. Queen Ranavalona I, who ruled from 1828 to 1861, rejected the British influence adopted by the previous rulers. She was especially hard on the missionaries. She did approve of the French, however, and allowed Jean Laborde, an engineer, to introduce Western technology.

Queen Ranavalona I

After the queen's death, Christianity returned—stronger than ever. In 1869, it became the official religion of the Merina kingdom. The weakness of the monarchs who followed—including Ranavalona's son, Radama II, who ruled from 1861 to 1863—paved the way for the French, who were anxious to gain control of the island.

The French enlisting natives of Madagascar to fight against rebels seeking independence, 1895

The French Colonial Era

The French had not kept their hands off Madagascar while the British were in favor, and in 1883, they began to attack the country's ports. The warfare lasted more than two years. When it was over, the French forced the Malagasy to accept a treaty making Madagascar a French protectorate. This meant that the island was protected by France—but, in fact, the Malagasy needed protection *from* France. The British were of no help, signing away their own interests in 1890. By 1895, the French were fully in charge, and in 1896, the country became a French colony. The Merina kingdom was at an end.

Madagascar was now ruled by a governor-general, Joseph Simon

Gallieni. His first move was to ban the use of English and make French the official language of the country.

Resistance

There was resistance to French rule from the beginning, but there was also resistance to Rainilaiarivony, the Merina general who dominated the other Malagasy peoples. A resistance movement called *menalamba* began. *Menalamba* means "outlaws" or "red shawls" in the Malagasy language, but the members of this movement were not common thieves. They were political fighters, determined to rid themselves of Rainilaiarivony.

Governor-general Joseph Simon Gallieni

Resistance to French colonization was vigorous and led by a group of well-educated Merina people. They formed a political group in 1913 known as Vy Vato Sakelika (VVS). Although it was a secret society, the French were aware of the opposition and aggressively worked to defeat it. Hundreds of VVS members were jailed by the French. But even as they tried to put an end to the VVS, the French realized that the Malagasy people were growing increasingly unhappy with French rule. Although the Malagasy were given few rights, they were expected to fight for France when World War I began in 1914. This treatment inspired the Malagasy to push for their own freedom.

Malagasy troops fighting for the French in World War II

The Malagasy worked on getting labor reform and equal rights. They saw these as the first steps toward full independence from France. But little progress was made until after World War II (1939–1945), when the French allowed a form of self-rule for the Malagasy.

Political parties then began to form. In 1946, the French changed Madagascar's status from a colony to an overseas territory, allowing the islanders to send representatives to the French government in Paris and to have a local government in Madagascar. But the island was in a state of political turmoil, trying to adjust to the many changes that were taking place after World War II. The way the country was being ruled, with both French and Malagasy governments having a say, did not please either side. Malagasy war veterans, especially, were dissatisfied with the treatment they received upon their return to the island, compared with the reception given to French people. By this time, political unrest had reached across all of Madagascar's people. The Democratic Movement for Malagasy Restoration (MDRM) had 300,000 members. It represented people from every ethnic group and social class across the island.

Resentment against the French came to a boil on March 29, 1947, when the people rose up in violent protest. Many Malagasy died in the hostilities that spread over one-third of the island—

estimates range from 11,000 to 80,000. Many thousands of others were brought to trial and convicted of various crimes. More than 5,000 people were imprisoned; a few were put to death.

Independence

The real move toward independence for Madagascar came nearly a decade later. As hard as the Malagasy themselves had fought to be free, the person who really set the wheels in motion was French president Charles de Gaulle. Within two years of his election as president in 1958, nearly all the French colonies gained their independence.

In 1956, a new political system gave the Malagasy more control. While the Merina, who lived in the highlands, had been the major power under the old system, the new structure favored the coastal people. After a brief period of self-rule under

President Philibert Tsiranana (pointing) at a ceremony in Paris granting Madagascar independence

France, a vote was held to move the country to full independence. On June 26, 1960, Madagascar finally gained its independence from France.

Independence did not put an end to the political divisions on the island, however. The country's first president, Philibert Tsiranana, wanted to remain closely tied to France and signed many agreements with France in order to keep that relationship.

This angered members of the opposition, who believed that all people deserved the same rights. They wanted to change the basic social structure of the country. Almost from the moment people began arriving on the island, a class structure of lower and higher classes had prevailed. With independence, some people saw an opportunity for the nation to get rid of the old system that made it impossible for a person to move beyond his or her class.

The First Republic

President Tsiranana seized the opportunity to create a government that favored his own political party. He put his friends into positions of power. But the country was governed very much along the structure that had been established by the French. The systems they introduced remained in place. At the time of independence, 67,000 French citizens were living in Madagascar. As the Malagasy took over the job of running the new nation, many French people left. The shift from French to Malagasy officials took place quickly. Within two years, most of the senior positions in important ministries had been taken over by Malagasy.

However, the French continued to dominate the educational system, and French culture was still taught in the schools. In 1972, 100,000 secondary-school students went on strike in protest. They wanted Malagasy teachers, and they wanted to learn about their own culture. The government responded harshly, closing the schools, arresting several hundred student leaders, and banning the demonstrations.

Meanwhile, the economy was slowing down, in part because of a great loss of cattle to disease. No one seemed interested in investing new money to build up the country's industry and create new jobs. There was growing ethnic anger and conflict between the highlanders and the *côtiers*—the people of the coast. Protests continued, and, in desperation, President Tsiranana dissolved the government on May 18, 1972, and turned over power to the army. The army was unable to solve the country's economic and ethnic problems, and turmoil continued. Finally, in 1975, a new head of state, Lieutenant Commander Didier Ratsiraka, was selected by the army. The period known as the Second Republic began.

Students parading in Antananarivo following President Tsiranana's resignation in 1972

The Second Republic

Ratsiraka was elected president for a seven-year term in a national referendum held on December 21, 1975. He planned to build an entirely new Malagasy society based on socialist principles. He virtually closed the country to outsiders, especially Westerners, and very few foreigners visited the island between 1975 and 1987. A new political party, the Vanguard of the Malagasy Revolution, was founded. It was named the

Demonstrators demanding
President Didier Ratsiraka's
resignation in 1991

Albert Zafy during the
presidential campaign
in 1992

government's party. All the ideas guiding the country were contained in a new charter known as the Red Book.

President Ratsiraka was an admirer of North Korea's president, who ruled with an iron fist and rigidly controlled his country's economy. But that system didn't work for either country. Faced with the difficult task of turning around Madagascar's economy, the new government made several very big and very costly mistakes. As conditions worsened, President Ratsiraka's popularity declined. He desperately tried to hold on to power and even rigged the voting to guarantee he would win, but the end of his reign was near. In 1992, a new constitution was written and new presidential elections were held.

On March 27, 1993, President Albert Zafy, the first new leader in seventeen years, was sworn in. The Third Republic began.

The Third Republic

The newly elected president didn't last long. President Zafy had inherited an economy that was in terrible shape. His hold on power was shaky—at one point, former president Ratsiraka even refused to move out of the presidential palace. President Zafy quickly found himself disagreeing with just about everyone who had a say in how the country should be run. The

International Monetary Fund (IMF) and the World Bank, which guarantee loans to needy countries, insisted on a complete overhaul of the economy, but President Zafy was afraid these changes would give too much power to outsiders.

When the issue of how the country should continue was put to a vote on September 5, 1996, Zafy was impeached. He resigned the next month, and in December 1996, Didier Ratsiraka was reelected president. He was the only leader who could get enough votes to win, and he was a familiar figure. Although he had made a mess of the economy in the past, he seemed to have learned from his mistakes.

Today, Ratsiraka is trying to open up the country to investments, trade, and development. One way he plans to do this to sell off the many businesses owned by the government, including the national airline, Air Madagascar; the telephone company, Telma; and the national oil company, Solima.

Didier Ratsiraka was elected president for the second time in 1996.

Ruling
Madagascar

CHAPTER

FIVE

66

THE PRESIDENT IS THE HEAD OF MADAGASCAR'S GOVERN-ment and is elected by all the people over the age of eighteen. The president shares power with the prime minister, but the prime minister is chosen by the parliament rather than being elected by the people. The prime minister then selects the twenty-eight members of the cabinet, called the Council of Ministers. The cabinet ministers oversee aspects of the government including agriculture, armed forces, environment, health, industry, justice, tourism, and transport.

The Executive Branch

The person nominated for prime minister must receive a majority of votes in the parliament, and must then be approved by the president. If the nominee does not receive support from the parliamentary majority, the president may choose anyone from parliament to serve as prime minister for one year.

Because of this government structure and the personalities of the men in power, the president is by far the most powerful political person in the country. Officially, however, the prime minister is responsible for the day-to-day running of the government. The president lives in the presidential palace on the outskirts of Antananarivo. It was built with the help of foreign aid.

The president is elected for a five-year term and may run for one additional five-year term. The Malagasy have come up with an informal division of power between the

Opposite: **The Presidential Palace**

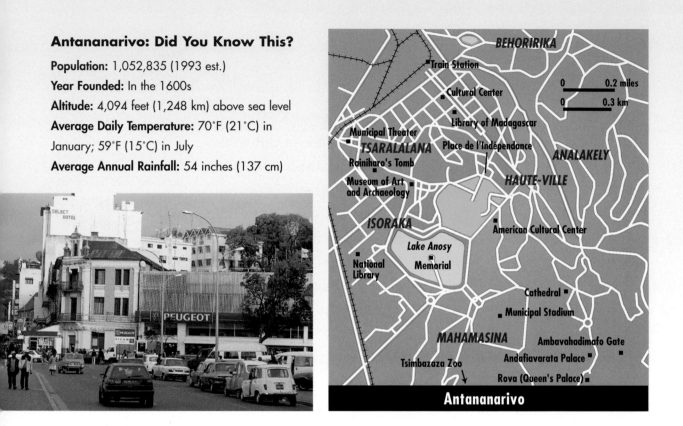

Antananarivo: Did You Know This?

Population: 1,052,835 (1993 est.)

Year Founded: In the 1600s

Altitude: 4,094 feet (1,248 km) above sea level

Average Daily Temperature: 70°F (21°C) in January; 59°F (15°C) in July

Average Annual Rainfall: 54 inches (137 cm)

Merina, who live in the highlands, and the côtiers, who live on the coast. If a Merina is elected president, the prime minister is chosen from the côtiers. If a côtier becomes president, the prime minister is chosen from the Merina.

The Legislative Branch

Parliament has two houses, the Senate and the National Assembly. The president has considerable power here too, choosing one-third of the members of the Senate; the rest are chosen by an Electoral College. The 138 deputies of the

National Assembly are elected by all the people to represent the areas they serve. The more highly populated regions have more deputies. This is similar to the House of Representatives in the United States. Members of parliament serve for a term of four years.

Government reaches the people through a series of local groups. There are 28 regions, called *faritany*; more than 100 departments, called *fileovana*; and nearly 1,000 communes, called *faribohitra*. This structure was created in 1994 to take power from the central government and give it to the various regions.

Government buildings lie behind the stadium in Antananarivo.

Antananarivo is built on steep hillsides.

NATIONAL GOVERNMENT OF MADAGASCAR

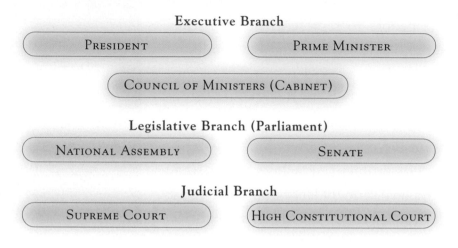

Executive Branch

PRESIDENT

PRIME MINISTER

COUNCIL OF MINISTERS (CABINET)

Legislative Branch (Parliament)

NATIONAL ASSEMBLY

SENATE

Judicial Branch

SUPREME COURT

HIGH CONSTITUTIONAL COURT

Public Health

Imagine driving down a road and suddenly finding the way blocked by a team of medical officers representing the Ministry of Health. "Take these pills," they say, "or you cannot travel any farther." You take the pills,

and a nurse gives you a small piece of paper with a number and the date stamped on it—proof that you took the pills.

In September 1999, everyone traveling in Madagascar had this experience, including the authors of this book. A dread disease called cholera had struck in the north of the country, and there was fear that it would spread to the south. Anyone traveling south from Antananarivo was faced with a barricade. Hundreds of people lined up, waiting patiently in the hot sun to reach the table where nurses were giving out the medicine. The lines were very orderly. Pregnant women were sent to a tent where they received special care.

Cholera is spread mainly by unclean drinking water. It can be fatal without prompt medical treatment. The cholera outbreaks are an indication of the lack of clean drinking water and the poor sanitation on Madagascar.

The Court System

Madagascar has an eleven-member Supreme Court, which settles disputes about the laws that govern the people. There is also a High Constitutional Court.

Provinces

Madagascar is divided into six administrative provinces: Toliara in the southwest; Fianarantsoa in the southeast, Antananarivo in the center, Toamasina in the northeast, Mahajanga in the northwest, and Antsiranana in the north.

Fokonolona

Traditionally, the Malagasy were governed on the village level through the *fokonolona*, a self-rule association. The fokonolona was made up of village elders and important people from the village. It was responsible for maintaining the peace of the community. It also looked after people who needed help—either financial help or just general help in day-to-day living and decision-making.

The fokonolona brought government right down to the level of the family. Meetings were held to discuss local issues, and the people tried to do this with the highest degree of cooperation. At these meetings, members made speeches known as *kabary*. These speeches were very beautiful and poetic, but they were often used to criticize someone in a roundabout fashion. Under King Adrianampoinimerina, the fokonolona was used to carry out the king's wishes. The traditional fokonolona system was revived in the 1970s and continues today.

A Land
of Farmers

MADAGASCAR IS A LAND OF FARMERS. MOST MALAGASY people live very much as their grandparents did. Nearly all the people grow rice on very small, irrigated plots of land, and many also grow cassava and other foods. Some cash crops, including coffee, sugarcane, vanilla, cloves, and sisal, are grown on the island. Cash crops are crops sold to other

Opposite: **Harvesting rice in the highlands**

Men harvesting sugarcane at a plantation

Sisal fibers drying in a field
near Tôlañaro (Fort Dauphin)

countries. Agricultural products account for 80 percent of the country's exports and employ 80 percent of the nation's labor force.

About 7.4 million acres (3 million ha)—or 5.2 percent of the total land area—is under cultivation. Most farms are just 3 acres (1.2 ha), and in the central highlands, irrigated rice plots average only 1.2 acres (0.5 ha). Malagasy also raise cattle, which they graze wherever there is open land. Half of Madagascar's land is used to feed livestock.

The economy is run largely by the government. In the 1970s, the Malagasy government bought up a large share of nearly all the important industries, including transportation, mining, manufacturing, and banking. The idea was to make the economy more Malagasy and less French. President Ratsiraka believed in centralizing all decision making. Firms that were not owned by the government were forced to buy and sell at government-controlled prices. The result was often inefficiency, which led to a lack of economic growth. The population was growing, but the economy was not keeping up with it.

Star Bottling Company

The thirst for soft drinks is almost universal, and in Madagascar, the Star Bottling Company quenches that thirst. Star is the local Fanta bottler and also supplies Coca-Cola and the popular Three Horses beers. Its factory, located in the industrial area of Antsirabe, is modern and completely self-sufficient. It has a conveyor system for recycling, in which used bottles are washed and inspected. Bottles that pass inspection continue on the conveyor line to the filling area, where they are filled, capped, and loaded into plastic crates for delivery to customers. The company makes its own colorful crates right on the grounds.

After nearly a decade under this system, the economy had sunk so low that President Ratsiraka began to turn certain industries back into private hands and reduce the government's role. This process has been slow, however, because few investors want to put their money into businesses that are going to be very slow to make a profit. The government has also taken on huge debts in the form of loans. The interest paid on these loans also hurts the economy.

Rice terraces

Rice, the principal crop of Madagascar, is grown on every available inch of land. The Betsileo people are considered the most efficient rice farmers, making the best use of very difficult, steep plots of land. They use a system of irrigation that carries water along a series of canals, often for a very great distance. Their rice fields are terraced—a series of small plots of land is carved out of a hillside, and each plot is separated from the next by a ridge of land that keeps the topsoil and water from running out. A group of terraces looks like a beautiful green checkerboard. Some are quite tiny, only a few square yards.

The tavy method of rice growing is practiced in the forested areas by the Betsimisaraka and Tanala people. This traditional method involves cutting down the smaller trees and brush and letting them dry on the field. Then, just before the rainy season, the field is burned. After the land has been cleared, it is planted with rice and corn. The land is used for crops for two or three years, and then it is left to recover and renew itself. It can take anywhere from ten to twenty years before the land can be used again.

Tavy has been declared illegal by the government because it destroys the land. It is still practiced, however, despite severe penalties that include imprisonment. The people depend on tavy because it allows them to plant faster-growing rice than can be grown in irrigated fields.

Tavy, the traditional slash-and-burn method of clearing land for farming, is illegal in Madagascar today.

What Madagascar Grows, Makes, and Mines

Agriculture

Paddy rice	2,600,000 metric tons
Cassava	2,450,000 metric tons
Sugarcane	2,200,000 metric tons

Manufacturing

Cotton cloth	25,000,000 metric tons
Refined sugar	89,474 metric tons
Cement	45,009 metric tons

Mining

Salt	80,000 metric tons
Chromite ore	74,000 metric tons
Graphite	13,900 metric tons

Zebu Cattle

The number of zebu cattle on Madagascar is roughly equal to the number of people. In 1990, the Food and Agricultural Organization of the United Nations estimated the island had 10.3 million cattle, 1.7 million sheep and goats, and 21 million chickens. Most of the smaller livestock is found on the plateau. Since a recent drought, however, the number of cattle has dropped considerably.

Cattle are grazed on any available land. To promote new growth, the farmers often burn the dry grasses. This adds to the overall problem of burning the land.

Zebu cattle have great curved horns and a distinctive hump to their backs. In Madagascar, as in much of Africa, owning cattle is a measure of wealth. Families in the south and west, where most of the cattle are raised, try to increase their herds as much as possible. In general, cattle are not raised for their meat but are used for religious sacrifice. When certain traditional religious celebrations take place, cattle are killed and eaten. Among the Bara,

Zebu cattle at a water hole

the Sakalava, and other groups in the south and the west, these ceremonial occasions take place so often that the people eat quite a lot of meat.

Otherwise, the herds just grow, much to the annoyance of the government, which would like to see more of the cattle in Madagascar used for meat or sold to earn money. The Sakalava, the Bara, the Tsimihety, the Mahafaly, and the Antandroy are the main cattle raisers of Madagascar. Among the Sakalava, who make up 6.2 percent of the population, the cattle in the most remote areas often outnumber the human population. The Tsimihety, who live in the north-central part of the country, are among the most isolated people on the island. They make up 7.3 percent of the population, and cattle are at the center of their culture.

Foreign Aid

Madagascar has a basic problem with its economy. The population is growing faster than the country can produce goods or crops for sale. Only 175,000 people—3.6 percent of the workforce—actually earn money. Nearly all the rest, 4.3 million people, are subsistence farmers who grow only enough food to feed their own families. This imbalance causes the country to keep getting deeper in debt with no plan to stop the endless cycle.

One way to stop this cycle would be to speed up development. To do this, the country needs money to invest in new industries. In 1999, the World Bank agreed to lend Madagascar U.S.$100 million. The money will be used for many projects—some directed by the government and others run by private citizens.

Until the 1980s, most foreign aid came from France and Japan. The United States began to give Madagascar substantial amounts in the 1990s, and by 1992, U.S. aid nearly equaled that given by France.

Vanilla

When you lick a scoop of delicious vanilla ice cream, do you ever wonder what makes it taste like that? Vanilla is a seed that grows on climbing orchid vines, and Madagascar used to be the world's main supplier. Before 1995, more than 80 percent of all the vanilla in the world came from Madagascar and the small neighboring islands of Réunion and the Comoros. It was Madagascar's most important export crop and cash earner.

Vanilla-growing areas are found along the east coast around Andapa, Antalaha, and Sambava, where the hot, moist climate is just right for this plant.

Vanilla is a difficult crop to grow on Madagascar because its flowers must be pollinated by hand. In Mexico, where the plants originated, birds and bees pollinate the vanilla, but none of the birds or bees in Madagascar seems willing. After pollination, it takes nine months for the seed pods to develop. When they are ripe, each pod contains tens of thousands of very small seeds. Harvesting the pods is just the beginning. Afterward, the pods are boiled and then kept very hot until they turn from green to a rich chestnut brown. Next, they are sorted by hand and grouped. Finally, they are ready to be packed and shipped. And where do they go? Ninety percent of the crop goes directly to the United States, where it is used to flavor ice cream. Vanilla is also used to flavor cakes and candy.

Vanilla production was introduced to Madagascar by French farmers who emigrated from the nearby islands. The greatest production was in 1988, when the island produced 1,500 tons. By 1993, the crop had declined to just 700 tons, and by 1995, to only 660 tons. Part of the problem was created when the Madagascar government taxed the farmers so heavily that they forced the price up too high. Other countries, including Indonesia, stepped in because they knew they could produce vanilla for less money. These new growers made it even harder for the Malagasy farmers to produce a crop at a competitive price. In addition to competition from Indonesia, which is now a major producer, there is another form of competition that doesn't depend on weather or farmland—synthetic vanilla. The synthetic flavoring, made in chemical plants in the United States and France, has taken a large share of the market. The vanilla grown on Madagascar, however, is still considered the best in the world.

Cloves

Spices are used around the world, and Madagascar was once the leading producer of cloves. It shipped tons of the tiny, fragrant buds around the world, especially to Indonesia. Although cloves are small in size and easily shipped, they are very valuable. But when Indonesia began its own clove production in the 1980s, the demand for Madagascar's crop suddenly plummeted. By 1993, the country was producing only half the cloves it grew only a few years earlier.

Fisheries

It's only natural that an island surrounded by rich fishing grounds would produce fish. Madagascar is a leading producer of shrimp, which is now the fastest-growing part of its agricultural production. Total fish production has increased dramatically since 1988, and much of this increase came from shrimp. The increase was made possible through the addition of 86,484 acres (35,000 ha) of swampland that had not previously been used for agriculture. Income increased more than ten times during this period. By 1993, the country was exporting 114,370 tons of shrimp annually. In 1999, the value of all the seafood exported was estimated to be U.S.$100 million.

A shrimp farm

Women fishing with baskets in rice fields

Men and women in Madagascar also catch fish with baskets. They cast their baskets in the rice paddies and use the baskets as strainers, letting the water run out and then gathering up the tiny fish.

Visitors

The number of people who visit Madagascar each year is quite small. In 1990, only 1,000 U.S. citizens made the journey. In 1997, 130,000 foreign visitors arrived on the island. That number includes businesspeople, people working on aid projects, and tourists. About 33 percent of the foreign visitors are French, many visiting their relatives, and 25 percent are from the neighboring island of Réunion. Germans make up about 18 percent of the visitors. Only 5 percent are U.S. citizens, including Peace Corps volunteers who help Malagasy teachers improve their English-teaching skills. Peace Corps volunteers also work in health programs aimed at preventing disease and improving nutrition. Madagascar also attracts an enormous number of scientists who come to study the natural environment. Other visitors include the many volunteers who come to help with environmental projects.

Despite its wonderful animals and plant life and its beautiful coastline, Madagascar has never developed as an important tourist destination. It has few facilities for tourists such as hotels and decent roads.

Tourists in Périnet Reserve

Working with a fossa in its natural habitat

Antaimoro Paper

A decorative paper made only in Madagascar is known as Antaimoro paper. The paper is made of pulp from a shrub that is soaked in a vat and pounded until it reaches the right consistency. The pulp is then applied to fabric stretched onto a frame and spread out into the shape of a sheet of notepaper. While it is still wet, wildflowers are pressed into the paper to form decorative borders or a pretty ornament on the cover of a folder. Then the paper is allowed to dry in the sun until it can be handled. It is quite sturdy and can be used as writing paper.

Crafts

The Andravoahangy Market in Antananarivo is the center for crafts. Here, objects made of local materials including wood and beautiful gemstones are sold. Madagascar solitaire sets, chess sets, Malagasy musical instruments, leather items, and inlaid wooden boxes are offered in the markets and along the roadside.

Inlaid wooden boxes are the specialty of the town of Ambositra. Using a technique called marquetry, woodworkers create a picture in colored woods. The pieces are fitted together like a jigsaw puzzle.

Madagascar's embroidery has a distinctive look and is easily recognized. The technique was introduced by the wives of

English missionaries and has become an important cottage industry. Malagasy women use embroidery to depict scenes from everyday life. They also embroider local flowers, birds, and lemurs on the fabrics, which are very colorful and very beautiful.

Hats made of straw or raffia are worn throughout the island. They are made by hand and come in an amazing variety of shapes and styles. Lambas, which are wraps worn by both men and women, and malabars, worn by men, are made locally.

Mining

Small amounts of minerals are found on Madagascar, but most deposits are not large enough to make commercial mining profitable. The biggest mineral reserves are of chromium and graphite, and these are being mined. Large reserves of bauxite in the southeast have not yet been worked, and conservation groups strongly oppose bauxite mining.

Small-scale mining of colored gemstones has taken place for many years. These mines can be very profitable despite their small size because gems bring high prices. Among the colorful and beautiful gemstones are sapphire, agate, beryl, quartz, garnet, amethyst, moonstone, tourmaline, and citrine.

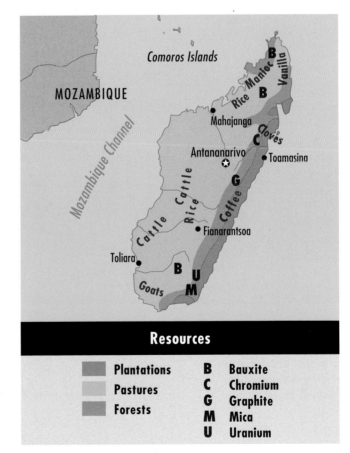

Resources

▓ Plantations	B	Bauxite
▓ Pastures	C	Chromium
▓ Forests	G	Graphite
	M	Mica
	U	Uranium

A husband and wife sift gravel at a sapphire mining camp, looking for gemstones.

One of the most beautiful and unusual gemstones found in Madagascar is the color-change garnet. Depending on the light, this gem can be a rich raspberry red or a greenish-blue. These garnets are highly valued in the jewelry industry in the United States and elsewhere.

In Madagascar, Merina jewelers polish and set colored gemstones in small workshops. The gem center for this trade is in the town of Antsirabe, where people sell gems on the street much as newspapers are sold in other cities. These dealers carry gems wrapped in small pieces of white tissue paper or arranged on cotton in little bamboo boxes. A group of two dozen gem dealers built their own stalls by Lake Andraikiba, on the outskirts of Antsirabe. The rutted dirt road leading to this gem market doesn't discourage visitors. Colored gemstones are used to make decorative objects such as eggs, spheres, marbles, and polished slabs.

Uncut gemstones

Malagasy Money

The unit of currency used in Madagascar is the Malagasy franc. One Malagasy franc contains 100 centimes. The value of the Malagasy franc is falling rapidly in relation to other world currencies, which makes imported goods even more expensive.

The paper money features scenes of daily life in Madagascar, including people with zebu cattle, handicrafts, the Queen's Palace, musical instruments, and women harvesting herbs. Notes come in amounts ranging from 500 francs to 25,000 francs.

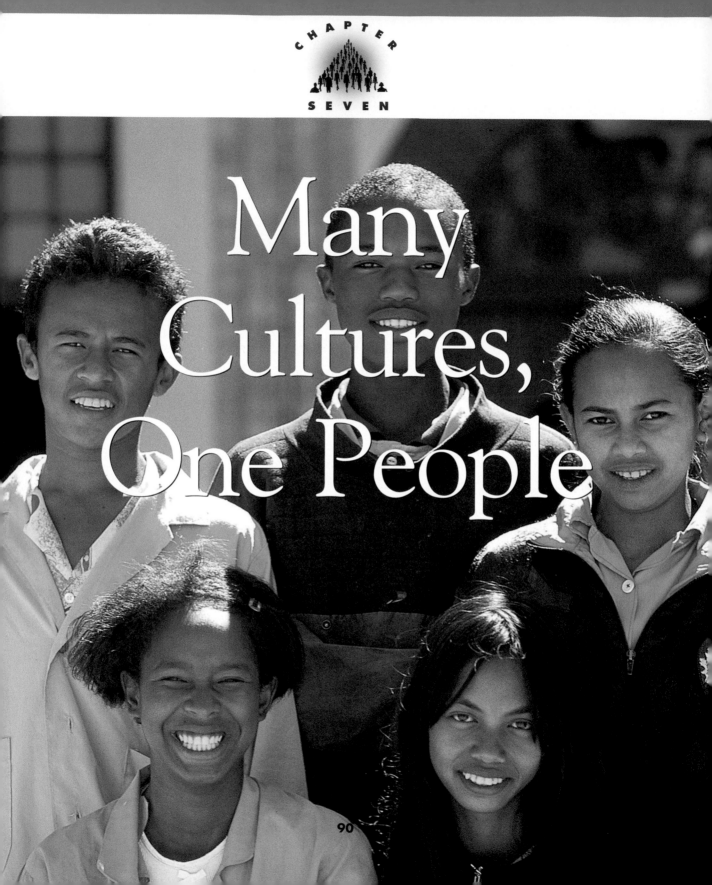

Many Cultures, One People

90

MADAGASCAR HAS ONE OF THE YOUNGEST POPULATIONS in the world. More than half its people are under the age of seventeen. The people are concentrated in certain parts of the island, especially on the plateau around Antananarivo and Fianarantsoa. In 1970, there were 7 million people. By 1996, that figure had nearly doubled, to 13,862,325.

A Malagasy woman has an average of six children. Today, more children survive to grow up and have children of their own, and the current population is expected to double again in twenty-two years. Still, life expectancy is just fifty-one years for men and fifty-three years for women. Only 3 percent of Madagascar's people are over sixty-five

Opposite: **Students in Antananarivo**

A Betsileo boy

A Family Album

The faces you see in Madagascar are a living family album that shows the results of ethnic mixing. Combinations of light and dark skin color and eye color, and straight or wavy hair, contradict everything we think we know about how genes behave. The people of Madagascar are of mostly Indonesian ancestry with some African and a little bit of French. The result is a wholly new people. Still, there are eighteen distinct ethnic groups among them, and each has its own history and culture.

Who Lives in Madagascar?	
Malagasy*	**98.9%**
Merina	27%
Betsimisaraka	15%
Betsileo	12%
Tsimihety	7%
Sakalava	6%
Antandroy	5%
Comorian	**0.3%**
Indian and Pakistani	**0.2%**
French	**0.2%**
Chinese	**0.1%**
Other	**0.3%**

*Individual Malagasy groups do not total 100%.

Each group lives in a fairly distinct part of the country, but now more people are moving to Antananarivo, where they mix with other groups. The groups also share cultural traits, especially respect for the dead. Ceremonies relating to ancestors are extremely important throughout the island. The groups share many other practices, such as circumcision of children, and have similar political views.

The most significant difference among groups is seen between the people who live on the central plateau, called "highlanders," and the people who live on the coast, known by the French word *côtiers*.

Highland schoolgirls dancing

The people are divided by geography and the different types of land and climate in each area. The Malagasy name for each group describes where the group lives or some special characteristic from the time they first came to the island.

Merina

The largest group and the most dominant people in Madagascar are the Merina. In Malagasy, *merina* means "elevated people." Their name comes from their location—high up on the plateau. They are also called "the people who can

Below left: **Population distribution in Madasgacar**

Below right: **A Merina doctor**

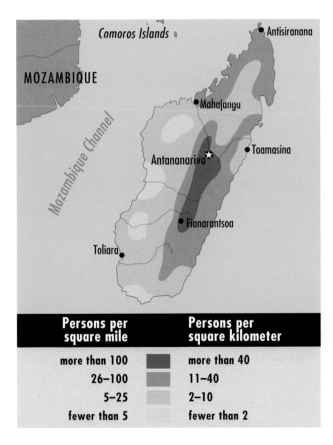

Persons per square mile		Persons per square kilometer
more than 100		more than 40
26–100		11–40
5–25		2–10
fewer than 5		fewer than 2

see far," which refers to their home on the plateau overlooking the sea. In appearance, the Merina have the lightest skin of all of the Malagasy and the most Asian features.

Traditionally, Merina men took a chief wife and lesser wives who were usually younger. Even after polygamy was legally abolished, some men continued this practice. And no matter what the law or religious practices of the day, the caste system remained the rule. People are ranked in one of three categories, mainly according to their skin tone. When Madagascar was a kingdom, the higher castes were people who had a relationship with the royal family. The stronger their ties to royalty, the higher their caste.

A Betsimisaraka woman

Lively Mix of People

The Betsimisaraka, whose name means "those who are inseparable," are the second-largest group on the island. The group grew after several smaller groups joined together in the early eighteenth century. The Betsimisaraka live on a long coastal strip on the eastern shore stretching all the way from Mananjary to Sambava.

The Tsimihety make up a little more than 7 percent of the population. Their name means "those who do not cut their hair." The Tsimihety live just south of the northern tip of the island. Their social

structure is less organized than that of any other group. Their lives revolve around the care of their large herds of cattle.

Although the Merina are the dominant culture of Madagascar today, the Sakalava people, who make up about 6 percent of the population, dominated much of the island in the sixteenth century. They are known as "the people of the long valley," and their territory is the largest on the island, covering much of the western half of Madagascar, stretching from the Onilahy River to Nosy Be. The Sakalava were led by

Population of Major Cities (1993 est.)

Antananarivo	1,052,835
Toamasina	127,441
Antsirabe	120,239
Mahajanga	100,807
Fianarantsoa	99,005

King Andriandahifotsy, who ruled over a large area. After his death, the next leader, Andriamandisoarivo, captured even more land and controlled important ports. This gave him contact with goods and ideas from the outside world. In spite of their huge kingdom, the Sakalava were conquered by the Merina in the nineteenth century.

The Sakalava are one of two groups considered the most "African" of all the Malagasy people because of their dark skin and their customs. The Sakalava, who live in the most remote areas, keep huge herds of zebu cattle. The Sakalava's semi-nomadic life—spent roaming their territory to graze their cattle—kept them from developing a close bond to their king. This made it possible for the Merina, a small group, to conquer the Sakalava.

Two other peoples, considered subgroups, live within the Sakalava region. They are the Makoa, whose ancestors were brought to the island from Africa as slaves, and the Vezo, fisherfolk who live in the southernmost part of the Sakalava territory, around Toliara.

The Antandroy are some of the poorest people in Madagascar.

Where People Live

The Antandroy, whose name means "people of the thorn bush," live in the spiny forest deep in the south and make up more than 5 percent of the population. This dry and desolate area has little to offer in the way of water or plants, and the Antandroy are among the poorest people of the island as a result. Unlike most Malagasy, they eat very little rice because they are unable to grow it in their area. They live instead on maize and cassava. They are semi-nomadic, moving from time to time in search of better living conditions.

A young Muslim boy

The Tanala people, whose name means "people of the forest," live in the rain forest around Ranomafana. The Betsileo, called "the invincibles," live on the central plateau around Fianarantsoa. They are rice farmers and skilled wood carvers.

The Antaimoro, known as the "people of the banks" or the "the people of the coast," live in a small section of the southeast coast. They are among the most recent arrivals and are closely connected to the Arab world of their ancestors. They practice old Islamic traditions and use Arabic script.

Many Cultures, One People **97**

A Mahafaly
tomb carving

The Bara people retain the most African features of any of the Malagasy. The meaning of their name is not known but the people are known for their practice of cattle rustling, called *dahalo*. Young men steal cattle to show they are ready for marriage. To the Bara, rustling proves a boy has become a man.

The Mahafaly, which means either "joyful people" or "makers of taboos," live in a small part of the southwest. They are among the most recent people to migrate to Madagascar, arriving less than 900 years ago. They managed to remain quite independent until the French colonized the island. Mahafaly are known for their colorful and elaborate tombs and for the wood carvings, called *aloalo*, used on their tombs to tell the story of their ancestors' lives.

The differences among the Malagasy people are a reflection of their original ancestry as well as the regions in which they now live. The range of environments on Madagascar shapes the lives of its people. Some people grow rice, some graze cattle, and some fish. Cultural practices have remained different because there is little connection or communication among the ethnic groups. Although they share one island, the people who live in different areas—the south or the north or on either coast—could be living in different countries.

Decision Making

The Malagasy talk over the problems of daily life as well as the
major issues to be decided. They have a number of names for the
different types of meetings they hold for these discussions. The
kabary was first used by Andrianampoinimerina. This is a public
meeting in which formal speeches are made, often using old

proverbs. There is a question-and-answer flavor to these meetings. The use of proverbs is a way of showing that the ancestors are being respected.

The basic family organization, called the *foko*, was once guided by the *fokonolona*, the village council of elders. Under Andrianampoinimerina, the fokonolona became an instrument for carrying out the king's wishes. In modern times, these powers have been taken over by the government and are carried out by elected and appointed officials.

Language

All of Madagascar's eighteen cultural or ethnic groups speak a dialect of Malagasy, so all of them can understand one another. The language comes from the Merina people and can be traced back to the eastern shores of the Indian Ocean. It is believed that the language arrived with the people, long ago. Traces of Bantu, a group of languages from central and southern Africa, are also present in Malagasy. Later, in the nineteenth century, Muslims from the Indian subcontinent joined the mixture. They too speak Malagasy. Even the arrival of Africans from the mainland has had very little impact on the Malagasy language.

Malagasy is spoken only in Madagascar, however, so the language used for business there is French. Madagascar's ties to France remained strong for the first twelve years after independence in 1960, both in business and in education. As a result, everyone in government speaks French. This use of French also gives Madagascar a language that is widely used outside the country.

Two Alphabets

The Malagasy language was first written down by Arabs in Arabic script, which is used throughout the Arab world. But when the Europeans arrived, they brought the Roman alphabet, which is used throughout North and South America and Europe. Today, the Antaimoro are the only Malagasy people who still use the Arabic script.

Madagascar's only French-speaking neighbors, however, are the islands of Réunion and the Comoros. France's other former colonies in Africa are on the west coast of the continent, thousands of miles away. The lack of a common language has kept Madagascar from developing relationships with its closer African neighbors, especially South Africa, which has the continent's biggest economy.

A small but growing number of Malagasy are learning English, and English-speaking people are very welcome in Madagascar. Many people associate them with the British missionaries who set up the first schools on the island. The U.S. Peace Corps has an English-language teaching program that instructs teachers in the language. A monument honoring U.S. president John F. Kennedy, who started the Peace Corps, stands on a main street in Antananarivo.

A road sign in Malagasy and French

Spiritual Life

RELIGIOUS BELIEFS ARE AT THE HEART OF MALAGASY culture. Traditional religious practices exist side by side with religions that came to the island from outside. Half the people—52 percent—follow only traditional religion, and 41 percent are Christians. The remaining 7 percent are Muslims, who live mainly in the northwest around Mahajanga. Most of the Muslims are descendants of people from the Comoros, where Islam is the official religion.

Opposite: **A bone-turning ceremony, in which ancestors are honored**

Traditional Beliefs

Traditional Malagasy belief centers on a supreme god known as *Zanahary* (The Creator) or *Andriamanitra* (Sweet Lord). A belief in the tie between the living and the dead is at the heart of the traditional religion. The ancestors, known as Razana, are treated with great respect and are considered very powerful. They are believed to influence the daily lives of the living. It is considered very dangerous to neglect the needs of the dead, for neglect can lead to great trouble.

Placing offerings at the tomb of King Andrianampoinimerina

Religions of Madagascar	
Traditional beliefs	52%
Roman Catholic	21%
Protestant	20%
Muslim	7%

The Ancestors

In Madagascar there is a saying, *Avy tsy nangeha nasesiky ny raza*, which means, "The ancestors come into our lives like guests who need no invitation." They must be kept informed about family events. The Merina and Besileo people do this in a ceremony called *famadihana*, which means "bone turning." The remains of a relative who has been dead for a long time are dug up and then passed around. This ceremony is carried out as often as possible—every year if the family can afford it. The ceremony is expensive because the whole village participates and food must be prepared for a large number of relatives and invited guests.

Since the time of burial, the silk lamba in which the body was wrapped will have disintegrated and must be replaced. The bones are wrapped in a new lamba and returned to the tomb. Sometimes they are moved to a new tomb. Afterward, the people at the ceremony talk about things that have happened since the last such ceremony. This is a very happy time for the Malagasy because they are fulfilling their obligation to their ancestors and because it brings them closer to their ancestors. It is considered a serious mistake not to perform this task if the family can afford it. Although the ceremony itself takes place only in the central highlands, respect for the dead is a practice shared by all the Malagasy people.

The Tombs

Because the Malagasy feel so closely connected to their ancestors' remains, they always try to bring the body home for burial if someone dies away from home. Otherwise, they believe the person's soul will wander the earth and not rest easily.

This connection with the dead has led to the construction of very elaborate tombs. These are small buildings that dot the countryside, especially in the south, where the Mahafaly and Antandroy people live. The construction of tombs is often the most important architecture in this region. People spend more time, money, and thought on the tombs than they do on building their own houses. Tombs, after all, must last much longer than one person's lifetime.

Some Mahafaly and Antandroy tombs are elaborately decorated.

An old wooden tomb carving

The tombs are considered the heart of the family, even more so than the homes of the living. Inside the tombs of the Merina, the bodies are wrapped in silk shrouds and kept on shelves. The tombs themselves are made of stone. Traditionally, the tombs of the Mahafaly were also stone, but nowadays they are more often made of concrete with glass windows. The Mahafaly also carve elaborate tomb posts, called *aloalo*, that mark the tombs. Standing as tall as 20 feet (6 m), each post is carved with the life story of the person buried in the tomb.

A nineteenth-century
illustration of a Catholic
mission school

More than 40 percent of Madagascar's population today are Christians. Those who follow the Christian religion are divided between Protestantism and Roman Catholicism. These divisions date back to the seventeenth century, when Protestant and Catholic missionaries made their first attempts to establish their religions on the island. Although these early attempts failed, the churches had begun to establish missions by the 1800s.

The first foothold was gained by the Reverend David Jones, who worked among the Merina. He brought more than religion—his small mission included a tanner, a carpenter, a blacksmith, a cotton-spinner, and a printer. The Merina proved to be eager students who embraced the new techniques and quickly applied them to their communities. The first mission school was opened in 1820 at the Palace of Andafiavaratra in Tananarive (now the capital city of Antananarivo). Just four years later, there were 2,300 students in mission schools, including more than 700 girls. The missionaries began translating the Gospels into Malagasy and by 1830, 3,000 copies of the New Testament had been printed.

Religion, as well as education, was set back after King Radama I died in 1828. His widow, Queen Ranavalona, hated all foreigners and stopped the missionaries' work. She rejected foreigners in general, except when it suited her purposes. For the next thirty years, the Malagasy people were largely without outside influence. During this period, however, a Frenchman named Jean Laborde was shipwrecked on the island. He had great technological skill, which the queen valued, and he paved the way for both the French takeover of the island and the arrival of French Catholic missionaries.

Queen Ranavalona broke treaties that had been signed with the British. She favored the French, who sympathized with her desire to resume the profitable slave trade that had been outlawed a few years earlier. A few British missionaries were allowed to stay because they taught the local people how to make European soap, which the queen preferred to the Malagasy soap. The British took advantage of this small opportunity and managed to stay on for five years. They were allowed to open new schools and to convert a few people to Protestantism.

But the queen was afraid that religious meetings and the ability to read and write threatened her power. She passed laws making it a crime for most ordinary people to learn to read and write. She expelled all the missionaries and ruled that the Malagasy could not become Christians or practice their religion if they had already converted. Finally, she cut off contact with the outside world by ending all foreign trade, including sending supplies to the nearby islands of Réunion and Mauritius. Madagascar was in nearly complete isolation.

When the queen died in 1861, Madagascar was thrown open to trade and to foreigners, and the missionaries were free to return. The Protestant and Catholic missionaries were

Important Religious Holidays

Easter	A Sunday in March or April
Ascension Day	A Thursday in May, 40 days after Easter
Feast of the Assumption	August 15
All Saints' Day	November 1
Christmas	December 25

fierce rivals—as much as the traders trying to secure their slice of the economic pie. Often the missionaries paved the way for the traders.

The role of churches during the latter part of the nineteenth century largely depended on the religion of the ruling queen. The queen, in turn, depended heavily on the prime minister, who had become very powerful. Each of the three queens who ruled until 1896, when France took over, was married to the prime minister. If the prime minister and the queen favored France, they chose Catholicism; if they preferred Britain, they chose Protestantism. Their choice of religion was closely related to the kinds of treaties Madagascar's ruling party was able to make with the French and British governments. Religion was not a private, personal choice, it was a matter of politics.

In 1869, when ruling Prime Minister Rainilaiarivony chose to be married in the Protestant Church, he gave up his Malagasy wife, even though they had had nineteen children together. Protestantism did not allow the Malagasy custom of polygamy, in which a man has more than one wife at a time.

Burning of the Talismans

Prime Minister Rainilaiarivony went much further than giving up his wife. He allowed the burning of the royal talismans of Imerina, also known as "the idols." In Malagasy they are called *sampy* and *ody*. There were twelve royal talismans, and when they were burned, the country appeared to be giving up its traditional religion. There was no outcry by the people, who had already moved in the direction of Protestantism. Some attended services willingly, while others were forced into churches, where they spent hours listening to sermons. It appears that the prime minister was trying to impress Queen Victoria of Britain with the religious belief of the Malagasy. This, he hoped, would gain the support of Queen Victoria and help keep out the French.

Traditional religious practices were now pushed aside in favor of civil law. Polygamy was outlawed, and anyone seeking a divorce had to go through a legal procedure.

Roman Catholic nuns in Antananarivo today

Additional religious sects came to the island, including Norwegian Lutherans, the Quakers, and American Lutherans, who set up a hospital at Fort Dauphin. The Catholic Jesuits also established themselves. The renewed acceptance of Western religions on the island meant that the mission schools could reopen. At the same time, Western medicine was introduced. These two institutions tied the Malagasy closely to the religions that supported them. Unfortunately, most of the these benefits were limited to the Merina. The Merina supported their church's activities with tremendous zeal.

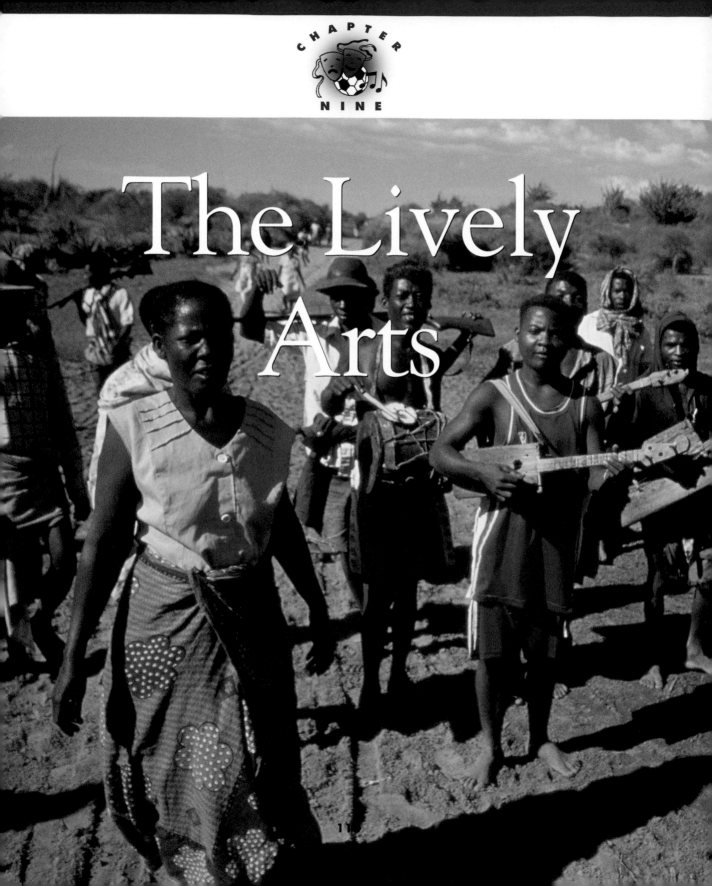

The Lively Arts

Music

WHILE MANY COUNTRIES HAVE DEVELOPED THEIR OWN styles of music, Madagascar has created its own unique musical instruments. They include the *marovany*, the *valiha*, and the *kabosy*, which belong to the family of instruments known as zithers and lutes. The marovany, a stringed instrument with a wooden sound box, comes from the zither family. The valiha has twenty-eight strings attached to a bamboo tube. The *sodina* is a Malagasy flute.

Madagascar's original music is based on complex rhythms that catch Westerners off guard. The rhythms have a different pattern than those of Western music. The music is traditionally played on Malagasy instruments, but the musicians often adapt its sounds to acoustic and electric guitars.

Since 1991, when Malagasy music was first recorded on compact disc in Madagascar, it has become well known outside the country. One album, the second volume of *A World Out of Time*, was nominated for a Grammy Award. This success led to more Malagasy artists recording music and touring the United States.

Opposite: **Local musicians with homemade instruments**

Malagasy musicians often adapt their traditional music to modern Western instruments.

Talking with Hanitra

One of the best-known musical groups in Madagascar is Tarika. The band, which has been called Madagascar's pop ambassador, adds electric guitars to the traditional instruments while keeping the original Malagasy sound. The singer who fronts the group, Hanitra Rasoanaivo, writes the lyrics and music for all the group's songs. She always sings in Malagasy.

"I write anything which hits me on the spot. We Malagasy are very attached to our land, our ancestors. Because Madagascar is an island, we have not been in touch with the rest of the world for a long, long time. South Africa was closed off. There is very little contact even now because language is a problem. Madagascar is a big country with a strong tradition. It's impossible to suppress this culture of being Malagasy. My music is something that I invented. I wanted the traditional instruments to survive."

Hanitra wants to unite the various parts of the island in her music by using instruments and themes from the south as well as from the Merina area, her homeland. In one dance, she imitates the elephant bird, which once lived in the south.

Above all, she says, "I believe very strongly in the spirit of ancestors. I want to find the origins of my people who came from Indonesia. We want to know where we came from, because we belong to the land of our ancestors."

Regis Gizavo is an accordion player who traveled to the New Orleans Jazz Festival in 1999. Dama Tambitamby is considered the musical poet of Madagascar. His popularity in Madagascar is compared to that of the Beatles in Great Britain. He is so popular that he was elected to Madagascar's parliament in 1993. One of the best-known Malagasy musicians is Paul Bert Rahasimanana, known as Rossy. He began performing music without any instrumental accompaniment at all, taking the beat from hand clapping. An annual music festival is held in May on Nosy Be.

Dance

The rhythm of Malagasy dance is driven by Malagasy music. Some dances are part of the culture of a specific group. The *salegy* is danced by the Sakalava tribes and combines Indonesian and African roots. The *tsapika* dance comes from the south of Madagascar; the *basese* from the north. The *sigaoma* is related to South African rhythms.

A traditional tribal dance

The Hira Gasy

The *hira gasy* is a spectacle that combines music, dance, and story-telling in one event. Colorful costumes set the scene for a troupe of performers. The troupes hold competitions to see who can create the best costumes and give the most exciting performance. The hira gasy begins with a *kabary*, a spontaneous speech on a particular theme. This theme is then taken up by the singers and dancers. The themes are well known to the performers because they focus on Malagasy beliefs such as keeping traditions, respecting parents, and the importance of honesty.

Malagasy Literature

The Malagasy tradition of telling stories aloud continues into modern times along with written forms of literature. The town of Fianarantsoa is now a literary center where a number of writers may be found, including Jean Ndema, Rainifihina Jessé, and Emilson D. Andriamalala. The spoken word is especially popular, especially the traditional *kabary*, which includes both speech-making and storytelling.

While kabary began as a form of political persuasion, it has changed into a popular form of entertainment. Great kabary speakers are fascinating in action, using all kinds of complicated language to delight the audience.

Proverbs, called *ohabolana*, are also important ways of sharing ideas and opinions. One is, "The zebu will lick bare stone and die in the earth of the place he loves." The very soil of Madagascar is loved by the Malagasy, and they feel strongly connected to it. Proverbs are best heard in the original Malagasy language because, like sayings around the world, they tend to lose a lot in the translation.

Fady

Fady describes a number of beliefs that guide the daily life of the Malagasy. Some fady consists of what we would call taboos—forbidden speech or actions. For instance, foods that you may not eat, including pork and goat, are called fady. Ways of living in society—what we might call manners or behavior—are also fady. Some people believe it is fady to relieve yourself inside a building.

The Queen's Palace

In a capital city with few landmarks, the Queen's Palace, also known as Palace of Andafiavaratra, was by far the most important building. Not only did it dominate Antananarivo's skyline with its extraordinary architecture, it also represented the cultural heart of the Malagasy people, especially the Merina. It was built on the site of the first mission school. The original palace, an enormous structure made of wood, was built by Frenchman Jean Laborde. Later, his wooden structure was completely covered in stone by James Cameron. Here, the remains of all the kings and queens of Madagascar were buried, making it the most sacred site in the nation. Together, they were known as the Rova. The palace housed a collection of antiques and gold and silver items that had been given to King Radama by Queen Victoria. Everything of historical value to Madagascar—both spiritual and financial—was housed at the Queen's Palace.

On the night of November 7, 1995, it was virtually all lost. A fire started in the early evening, first catching the brush around the palace, then burning the wooden structure and consuming almost everything inside it. This national tragedy was made even worse when the people learned that the fire had been set deliberately. No one knows exactly why, but in the end, it doesn't matter. The Malagasy lost a huge piece of their own history. Several governments as well as a branch of the United Nations have offered financial help, but money cannot make up for this loss.

Certain days are set aside as fady for specific activities. These rules are called *vintanta*, which has to do with time and destiny. The Malagasy believe that each day of the week has certain qualities. Some days are good for funerals, and other days are good for weddings. Some days are considered "easy" while others are "hard." These days may be different from group to group. For example, the Merina do not hold a funeral on Tuesday, because they believe this will cause someone else to die. Children learn all of these rules from their parents and other relatives.

Unique
Island Life

LIFE ON AN ISLAND IS A VERY SPECIAL KIND OF LIFE. IN Madagascar, where there are few tourists or other visitors, change comes slowly. The Malagasy follow their ancestral traditions, eat the same food as their grandparents did, and dress very much like them, too. Except for Antananarivo, the towns are still quite small. When young people grow up and marry, they live near their parents and near their ancestors' graves.

Schooling is compulsory for a period of five years. Only about 75 percent of the children actually attend primary school, however, and as few as 14 percent go on to secondary school.

Opposite: **Travel by pousse-pousse**

Primary school students and their teacher

There is very little industry or business in Madagascar, and the amount of land is limited. This combination will be a serious problem for the next generations as they try to grow food or look for work.

Getting Around

Most people stay close to home. Travel between towns and cities is difficult in Madagascar because the roads are poor. The island has many small airports, however, so businesspeople travel by air from city to city.

The streets of Antsirabe are crowded with *pousse-pousses*—vehicles much like rickshaws. A rickshaw is a small, two-wheeled carriage with a bench and two long poles

The streets of Antsirabe are crowded with colorful pousse-pousses.

extending from the front. The power is supplied by a person who stands between the poles and pulls the rickshaw. Rickshaws are a traditional means of transportation in China. They came to Madagascar in 1895 with the Chinese laborers brought in by the French to build the roads and railways.

In Antsirabe, pousse-pousses are a major form of transportation. Women go shopping for food in the local market and arrange with a pousse-pousse driver to pick them up at the market entrance. Businessmen with briefcases use them to get to their appointments. There is little public transportation in the town.

Taxi-Brousse

Outside Antananarivo, nearly everyone travels in a *taxi-brousse*, or country taxi. The taxi-brousse, which is usually a minivan, is a familiar sight, crammed full of people, with all sorts of luggage tied onto the roof. Suitcases, sacks of rice, bicycles—just about everything imaginable—may be found on top of a taxi-brousse.

Travelers in a truck watch a taxi-brousse that is stuck in the loose sand of the roadside.

Unique Island Life **119**

Small Business

With so few ways to earn money, some young people have followed their elders and started to make objects for sale. Along the roadside, children make and sell toy trucks. They are models of the real trucks that pass by every day delivering Coca-Cola and beer. Even the familiar Coca-Cola script is faithfully copied.

The Staff of Life

The most important food in Madagascar is rice. A day without rice is simply not a possibility for the Malagasy. The foods eaten with the rice are of much less importance. The typical dish consists of a huge mound of rice with a side dish of vegetables cooked in water. The vegetables are used somewhat like seasoning, almost like ketchup on french fries. The average Malagasy eats more rice than anyone else in the world,

including the Chinese. Each Malagasy eats, on average, 348 pounds (158 kg) of rice a year. As the population grows, the demand for rice grows, too. Each year, the demand for rice increases by as much as 30,000 tons.

Madagascar must sometimes import rice to meet this demand. In 1982, the nation imported 350,000 tons of rice; in 1987, five years later, it imported only 106,000 tons. But this drop didn't mean that there was enough rice to go around that year. It meant that many people were too poor to buy imported rice and had to eat other starches instead, including potatoes, maize (corn), sweet potatoes, and cassava.

The national costume of Madagascar is the *lamba*. The lamba is a length of fabric that can be worn in many ways, by both men and women. It is most often worn as a shawl, draped loosely over one shoulder or worn around the shoulders and draped over the head. Wrapped around the body and tied into a sling, it can be used to carry a small child. Sometimes a

This mother is carrying her infant wrapped in her lamba.

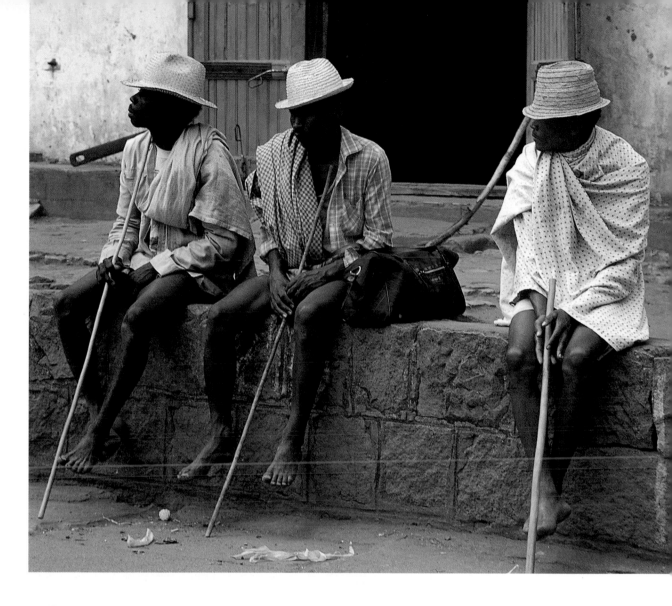

Malagasy proverb is printed on the hem. When the cloth is worn with one end falling along the right side of the body, it means that the person is in mourning, and the lamba is known as *lamba maitso* which means "green cloth." Red lambas are worn on special occasions and show that the person is someone in authority. The lamba began with the Merina but is also worn by the Sakalava and Antakarana.

These men wear their lambas over their shoulders. Many people go barefoot in Madagascar.

Houses

Traditional houses are built in a wide variety of styles and use various building materials. Because the climate varies so much around the island, each region needs a different kind of house. On the coast, houses are built of materials suitable for the warm climate, such as palm fronds. On the central plateau, where the weather is quite cold at night, especially in winter,

Wooden houses in a highland village

houses are usually made of brick. One of the most unusual forms of housing are the two-level brick homes found in the center of Madagascar. Many of these are trimmed with wood.

Two-level brick homes trimmed with wood

Making Bricks

The use of bricks for housing is one of the most unusual aspects of Malagasy culture. The brick-making industry was started by James Cameron, who came to Madagascar from Scotland in 1825. Bricks took the place of the wood that had been used for houses. The effect of the extensive cutting of the forests to build houses and the burning of fields to plant rice was already being felt. The boundary of the forested land was rapidly being pushed to the east. The brick making helped to slow down the loss of the forest around Tanarive (present-day Antananarivo).

Today, bricks are made throughout the central plateau, usually in the fields where rice is grown. The same earth is suitable for both, but once a field is used to make bricks, it cannot be used to grow rice.

Soccer and other ball games are popular in Madagascar.

Sports

Soccer is popular with boys throughout Madagascar and is played on fields in every town. Often, the boys make a soccer ball out of tightly rolled bundles of newspaper tied together and pulled into shape with string. Local competitions are held in the larger towns each week, usually on Sundays. Soccer is a popular spectator sport in Madagascar, and a local soccer game is often the major social activity of the week. In farm areas, games are played on the rice paddies. When they are dry, they make good, flat playing surfaces.

Volleyball and basketball are growing in importance. Girls and boys play together on outdoor courts on vacant fields. Basketball is popular because it allows boys and girls to compete equally and is not as rough as soccer or rugby, another favorite.

Games

Malagasy of all ages like to play *fanorana*, which is considered the national game. It is a much more complicated version of checkers, played on a square board marked with lines that form squares and triangles. Each player has five game pieces, which may be stones or rocks of a certain color. One player moves a piece along the lines of the squares and triangles until it bumps into another player's piece. The first player then jumps over that piece and claims it.

Katra, another board game, requires players to move small stones around a board until one player has captured all the pieces. It is played all over Africa, too.

In 1997, Madagascar hosted the Third Francophone Games in Antananarivo. The Francophone Games are a series of sports and cultural competitions. Athletes and artists from French-speaking countries around the world compete in events and contests ranging from boxing, soccer, judo, and women's basketball to traditional dance, storytelling, photography, and sculpture.

The Timeless Country

The gentle character of the Malagasy people and their genuine warmth are rare and unique. There is a sense of timelessness about Madagascar—the feeling of a place frozen in the past. This feeling comes from the houses without windows, the barefoot people, and the tiny shops that jostle for space along the roadway. It comes from the rice fields across the street from the international airport, and the gentle lemurs for which the island is known. It also comes from the strong connection that the Malagasy people maintain with their families, their ancestors, and their history.

Timeline

Malagasy History		World History	
People from Indonesia begin arriving on Madagascar.	About A.D. 1	2500 B.C.	Egyptians build the Pyramids and Sphinx in Giza.
		563 B.C.	Buddha is born in India.
		A.D. 313	The Roman emperor Constantine recognizes Christianity.
Arab traders arrive on Madagascar.	900s	610	The prophet Muhammad begins preaching a new religion called Islam.
		1054	The Eastern (Orthodox) and Western (Roman) Churches break apart.
		1066	William the Conqueror defeats the English in the Battle of Hastings.
		1095	Pope Urban II proclaims the First Crusade.
		1215	King John seals the Magna Carta.
		1300s	The Renaissance begins in Italy.
		1347	The Black Death sweeps through Europe.
		1453	Ottoman Turks capture Constantinople, conquering the Byzantine Empire.
		1492	Columbus arrives in North America.
Diego Dias, a Portuguese explorer, is the first European on Madagascar.	1500	1500s	The Reformation leads to the birth of Protestantism.
British traders and colonists arrive.	1600s–1700s		
Étienne de Flacourt builds Fort Dauphin.	1648		
French settlers flee Madagascar.	1669		
Andrianampoinimerina unites the Merina people and rules them.	1787–1810	1776	The Declaration of Independence is signed.
Radama I rules the Merina kingdom, conquers the Betsileo and Sakalava people, and welcomes European traders and missionaries.	1810–1828	1789	The French Revolution begins.
The first mission school opens.	1820		
Queen Ranavalona I expels Europeans from Madagascar.	1828–1861		
King Radama II reopens Madagascar to British and French traders and missionaries.	1861–1863		

Malagasy History

General Rainilaiarivony gains power as prime minister and becomes the husband of the next Merina queens.	1863
Christianity becomes the official religion of the Merina kingdom.	1869
Madagascar becomes a French protectorate.	1885
Madagascar becomes a French colony.	1896
Merina people form Vy Vato Sakelika (VVS), a secret political group.	1913
France grants Madagascar limited control of its own government.	1945
Madagascar becomes a French overseas territory.	1946
Malagasy people revolt against the French.	1947
Madagascar becomes a self-governing state in the French community.	1958
Philibert Tsiranana is elected president.	1959
Madagascar becomes an independent nation called the Malagasy Republic.	1960
Tsiranana resigns; army officers take control of government.	1972
Didier Ratsiraka becomes head of the government; multiparty politics are banned; Malagasy Republic becomes Madagascar.	1975
The government buys up major portions of the economy.	1975–1979
Ratsiraka is elected president.	1982
The ban on multiparty politics ends.	1990
Ratsiraka turns the government over to Albert Zafy.	1991
The government writes a new Constitution.	1992
Zafy is elected president.	1993
Zafy is impeached by the National Assembly.	1996
Ratsiraka is again elected president.	1997
The World Bank agrees to lend Madagascar $100 million.	1999

World History

1865	The American Civil War ends.
1914	World War I breaks out.
1917	The Bolshevik Revolution brings Communism to Russia.
1929	Worldwide economic depression begins.
1939	World War II begins, following the German invasion of Poland.
1957	The Vietnam War starts.
1989	The Berlin Wall is torn down, as Communism crumbles in Eastern Europe.
1996	Bill Clinton is reelected U.S. president.

Fast Facts

Official name: Republic of Madagascar

Capital: Antananarivo

Official language: Malagasy

Antananarivo

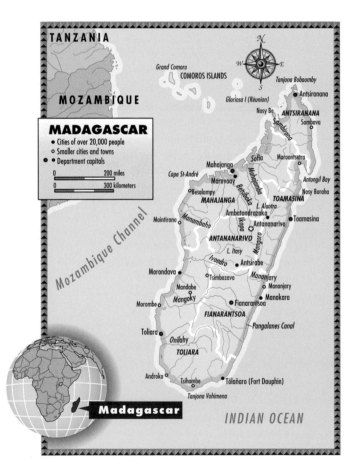

Madagascar's flag

Rice fields

Official religion:	None
Year of founding:	1960
National anthem:	*Ry Tanindrazanay Malala O (Our Beloved Country)*
Government:	Federal republic
Chief of state:	President
Head of government:	Prime minister
Area:	226,660 square miles (587,004 sq km)
Dimensions:	East–west, 360 miles (579 km); north–south, 976 miles (1,571 km)
Latitude and longitude of geographic center:	20° South, 47° East
Land and water borders:	Located in the Indian Ocean off the southeast coast of Africa, with Mozambique to the west across the Mozambique Channel and the Comoro Islands to the northwest
Highest elevation:	Maromokotro, 9,436 feet (2,876 m) above sea level
Lowest elevation:	Sea level along the Indian Ocean
Average temperature extremes:	84°F (29°C), in December along the coast; 5°F (–15°C) in July in the mountains
Average precipitation extremes:	128 inches (325 cm) of rainfall on the east coast; 14 inches (36 cm) of rainfall in the southwest
National population (1998 est.):	14,463,000

Tsingy de Bemaraha

Population of largest cities (1993 est):		
Antananarivo	1,052,835
Toamasina	127,441
Antsirabe	120,239
Mahajanga	100,807
Fianarantsoa	99,005

Famous landmarks:
▶ *Ankarana Special Reserve*
▶ *Berenty Reserve*
▶ *Great Spiny Desert*
▶ *Pangalanes Canal*
▶ *Périnet Special Reserve*
▶ *The Rova (King's Palace)*, in Ambohimanga
▶ *The Rova (Queen's Palace)*, in Antananarivo
▶ *Tsingy de Bemaraha Strict Nature Reserve*
▶ *Tsimbazaza* (zoo, museum, and botanical garden), in Antananarivo

Industry: Food processing is Madagascar's major manufacturing activity, with rice mills and sugar refineries turning out large amounts of goods. Other manufactured products include cotton cloth, soap, wood, and paper pulp. More than half of Madagascar's industries are located in or near Antananarivo. Mining remains an underdeveloped industry. However, the most important mining products are salt, chromite, and graphite, as well as gemstones such as quartz, amethyst, and garnets.

Currency: Madagascar's basic unit of currency is the Malagasy franc. In early 2000, U.S.$1 = 6,631 Malagasy francs.

System of weights and measures: Metric system

Currency

Malagasy students

Literacy (1990 est.): 80 percent

Common Malagasy words and phrases:

Aiza . . . ? (ize)	Where is . . . ?
Aza fady. (azafAD)	Please *or* excuse me.
haninai (an)	food
Iza no anaranao? (eeza nanARanow)	What's your name?
Manao ahoana (mano OWN)	Hello
Mba ampio aho! (bampeewha)	Please help me!
Mila . . . aho. (meel . . . a)	I want . . .
Misaotra. (misOWtr)	Thank you.
mofo (moof)	bread
Ny anarako . . . (ny anArakoo)	*My name is . . .*
Ohatrinona? (ohtrEEn)	How much?
rano (rahn)	water
ronono (roonOOn)	milk
trano (tran)	house
vary (var)	rice
Veloma. (velOOm)	Good-bye.
vohitra (voo-itra)	village

Famous Malagasy:

Andrianampoinimerina (d. 1810)
First king, 1787–1810

Radama I (d. 1828)
King, 1810–1828

Ranavalona I (d. 1861)
Queen, 1828–1861

Didier Ratsiraka
President, 1975–1992 and 1996–

Philibert Tsiranana (1910–1978)
First president, 1960–1972

Paul Bert Rahasimanana (Rossy)
Musician

Hanitra Rasoanaivo
Musician

Dama Tambitamby
Musical poet, politician

Didier Ratsiraka

To Find Out More

Nonfiction

▶ Bradt, Hilary. *Guide to Madagascar.* 5th ed. Old Saybrook, Conn.: Globe Pequot, Bradt Publications, 1997.

▶ Bradt, Hilary, Derek Schuurman, and Nick Garbutt. *Madagascar Wildlife: A Visitor's Guide.* Old Saybrook, Conn.: Globe Pequot, Bradt Publications, 1996.

▶ Heale, Jay. *Cultures of the World: Madagascar.* Singapore: Times Books International, 1998.

▶ *Madagascar in Pictures.* Rev. ed. Visual Geography Series. Minneapolis: Lerner Publications, 1988.

▶ Stevens, Rita. *Madagascar.* Places and Peoples of the World. New York: Chelsea House, 1988.

CD-ROM

▶ *Microsoft Encarta Africana: The Encyclopedia of Black History and Culture.* Microsoft, 1999.

Music

▶ *A World Out of Time*. Vols. 1, 2, and 3, *Music of Madagascar*. Shanachie Recordings, 37 East Clinton St., Newton, NJ 07860 (800) 497-1043.
Sales of this CD benefit the Madagascar Fauna Group.

Websites

▶ **Encarta Online Deluxe**
http://encarta.msn.com
An encyclopedia of Africa with articles and photos on Madagascar; includes excellent links.

▶ **Madagascar: A World Apart**
http://www.pbs.org/edens/
madagascar/eden.htm
A natural history of Madagascar that discusses the environment, conservation, and other related issues; includes visuals.

Embassy

▶ **Embassy of Madagascar**
2374 Massachusetts Avenue N.W.
Washington, DC 20008
(202) 265-5525
http://www.embassy.org/madagascar/

Index

Page numbers in *italics* indicate illustrations.

Meet the Authors

HEN ETTAGALE BLAUER AND JASON LAURÉ TRAVELED to Madagascar, they were both astonished and delighted with the country. "Madagascar is unlike any of the eighty countries I have been to," says author and photographer Jason Lauré. "I often felt I was traveling in South America instead of Africa because of the way people live, the dusty streets, the straw hats they wear, and their clothes. The country really seems to be floating out in the middle of nowhere."

Author Ettagale Blauer was amazed at the way Antananarivo, a city of more than 1 million people, functioned without a single working traffic light. "We could have driven ourselves around because we both speak enough French to get by, but we

would never have understood how to negotiate around the cars in the middle of the intersections. There is a sense of courtesy here that is something wonderful to experience. And of course we would have been lost once we left the capital since we don't speak Malagasy."

Both authors were continually impressed with the skill of the craftspeople who turn so many aspects of daily life into delightful objects—such as the tin plaques that look like the familiar taxi-brousses and the finely inlaid wooden boxes with scenes of country life. The statistics about rice consumption came to life when they saw the rice fields occupying every available inch of land on the highlands. "Although Madagascar is best known for its lemurs, it really should be appreciated for its people," they conclude.

Photo Credits